REMEMBRANCE

A LIFE IN REVIEW

OTHER BOOKS BY:

J.S. Schmidt

Learn To Be Still

Roses and Thorns

The Entwining

THIS BOOK IS DEDICATED TO:

Jeanne, my little sister; who has been so many different things in my life. These are a few of them: Sister, Friend, Adversary, Confidant, Companion, Grief Counselor, Technical Advisor. It's amazing to find all of these things in one spirit; one beautiful blue-eyed spirit.

CONTENTS

INTRODUCTION

W *hy do so many of us believe the answers to all our questions about life, lie somewhere in the future? Why do we have the ability to remember the past if it is truly irrelevant, as so many of us believe? Are we drawn to our memories because they are without ambiguity; because they are safe? Do most of us only revisit happy memories and happy places in our past life? Are memories packed with hidden knowledge that can help direct our future?*

If you believe there's nothing in your past that you don't already know, or that it's all set in stone and nothing can change any of it; I think you might be surprised at the things you could discover waiting there to be uncovered.

When I began to sort through the wreckage of my life, following the murder of my son, Ethan, the last thing I wanted to think about was the happy life I had known while he was in it. At that point, I couldn't see a future for myself and when I tried, I could only see gray, thick, fog.

At that time trying to live in the present was nearly unbearable. So, where do you place the focus of your thoughts when you can't see the future and the past and present only cause you more pain? The only place I found comfort at that time, was in Jesus. When the peace He gave me settled in my heart, I began to rebuild my life. I believe, as Matthew 7:24~27 says in the parable of the wise and foolish builders, that a house (life) must have a firm foundation, so I began to rebuild my life on the Rock (Jesus). I began at the beginning, in the past, and I discovered many things. I discovered things about myself and my relationships, my mistakes, things about life, truth and misconceptions.

I realized I was observing these things in my past with new eyes and a new and entirely different understanding. The miraculous thing is that in spite of acknowledging my mistakes and failures, I now perceive my life as wonderfully gratifying and I have more love for myself as a human being than I have ever had. Because I take this walk, through life, with Jesus and He reveals it to me through His eyes, His perception of me, I no longer focus on my failures. I see them, but I don't judge them or myself. I only feel Christ's love for me. My mother once told me that a friend of hers often said: "I can't wait to get to heaven, because God isn't as hard on you as people are!" I realize now how true that is. My walk through the past continues as I move into the future with clarity and purpose. I never walk alone, Jesus is always right there beside me and that gives me strength, hope, and courage to face whatever the future may bring.

If you have read my other books, I am honored; but I want to explain why I repeat in some form or other events that I've already covered. Many of these events continue to evolve as time passes. I thank you in advance for reading this book and for letting me share my remembrances with you.

- J. S. Schmidt

1

SWEET HOLY SPIRIT

I have discovered if I try to decide what a book will be about before I write it, I get about half of the chapters written and then realize it's really about something else; so it makes more sense for me to write the introduction after the book has revealed it's identity to me. I'm not sure it's usually done that way, but I think it's important to let the book develop itself. When I write and realize those times that the Spirit has taken over; I just try to keep up and write what I'm hearing. In those instances, I'm no longer thinking what I write; I just hear it. It seems I always have a "ghost writer", but in this case, it's the Holy Ghost.

This book began as a compilation of the amazing spiritual experiences I've had in my life; many but not all of these things occurred after my son's passing. As I moved through the initial stages of grief, I began to look back at my life for a number of reasons. I wanted to see if I could find other similar experiences that I had simply explained away. Instead of being about my spiritual experiences, this book when I thought I had finished writing it, was actually more about the "life review" I have been conducting for at least the past three and a half years. The chapters I wrote about these spiritual occurrences are being developed into another book that I hope to publish as my fourth book. I believe this review is far from over. To this point my life review has revealed many things to me and it has released me from my natural inability to recognize and accept my mistakes and failures and my responsibility for them. It has been a fascinating and bolstering experience and a journey I am pleased to have undertaken; it has answered so many of the enduring questions I had about life and I am learning to see myself, and know myself, as God sees me. That in itself is an astonishing experience.

This life review, I've undertaken is an ongoing thing; how long it will take to complete, I can't begin to say. It happens randomly, in no particular order. A persistent thought or memory comes to me and I examine it as fully as I can; writing what it reveals to me.

Spiritual signs are not usually recognizable to our human senses; they must be seen, felt and heard with spiritual senses. I hope some of that feeling comes across as you read things about me, my life and my transformation of consciousness, since I lost my son. Many of these things seem so ordinary, but the work of the Holy Spirit is embedded in them. It is my task to write about them in such a way that those who read my words, will be able to see beneath the ordinary appearance, to the spiritual energy that pulses at a lower depth. I hope I have been able to do that effectively.

I am so honored and blessed when someone takes time to read my books; some people tell me they've read them more than once and that blesses me tremendously. Thank you for devoting some of your time and attention to reading about my journey; I have a deep-seated desire to share it with others. I wish you God's peace, comfort and joy as you live your own story.

- J.S. Schmidt

2

LETTING GO

$\mathcal{I}$had the thought this morning, as I was brushing my teeth: "What if my life review gets bad reviews?" That is, what if sharing my personal search for meaning in the past, is badly received, or what if it's rejected entirely?

My next thought was: Who cares? Doesn't matter! I'm doing what I'm led to do. The life review itself is for my own personal reflection and growth. I share it on the chance that it might trigger someone else to conduct a life review of their own; or that it might bring a memory of something unresolved that needs resolution, in order to grow and progress.

There is always risk in putting yourself out there in any form; that is a portion of my aversion to Facebook, etc. People can be vicious in their rejection of someone else's opinions, actions or conclusions. I am only presenting my personal truth, that has become clear to me through the spiritual transformation that occurred after my son's passing. You can argue with anything or everything I say, but you can't change my truth. If it doesn't happen to correlate with yours, then I will wish you well on your own path as I continue traversing my own.

Sometimes, I will have the recurring thought to send my book to someone I know, who didn't ask for it. I act on recurring thoughts, because I believe they are spiritually significant. There have been times that I received a message thanking me for sharing the book and sometimes I hear nothing from the one I sent it to. As they say, silence speaks volumes. There isn't a verbal rejection, but it comes through loud and clear in the silence.

That's okay, because one's initial reaction isn't always the final reaction. I know I have said what needed to be said and perhaps just one little part of that will touch them at some later time and something will be moved forward, or revealed in their personal spiritual process. If that does happen, I celebrate it. If it doesn't, perhaps it still could. I am at peace that I followed the spiritual guidance I perceived.

About a year after Ethan's life was taken, I reached out to the family of the other innocent victim of the tragedy that changed so many lives. I sent a card and letter to the parents of the woman who was also murdered. I never received a reply and that's okay. I was acting on a recurring thought I'd had for several months, before I sent the card and letter. When I acted on those thoughts, they went away; even though no one responded. Sometimes you have to do the right thing, even if it only impacts you.

I don't write books to make money; money is nice, but it isn't my motivation. I write because I believe many of my words are inspired by the Holy Spirit and I believe there is a very good chance they can impact the lives of other people who read my books. Writing is my way of reaching out. I want to release what I've been given through the Spirit, so it can touch as many others as possible. What we release, comes back to us in amazing increase. I hope there will be many more books to write; time will tell.

3

SWEET INSPIRATION

I have often heard songwriters explain how they create their work; the way I write is very similar. I don't choose the topics; they choose me. I don't decide that today I'll write about this and tomorrow, I'll write about that. There is no plan. I don't begin with a title or an outline of chapters. The books I have written so far are compilations of thoughts and reflections on various topics. I would call them spiritual reflections that could be considered devotionals. I write chapters that tell an individual story or recollection or that carry a single thought. When I get the feeling, I've written all there is that needs to be included in the book, I stop. I look back through what I've written and see what appears to fit together and that becomes the book. In the beginning I have no idea how many chapters I will write and sometimes I think I'm finished and out of nowhere the inspiration comes to write more. I only know it's truly finished when nothing else presents itself to be written.

I don't schedule my writing time; I write when I'm inspired to write a specific thing. If I try to write and there's no inspiration, I just sit there looking at a blank sheet of paper, with absolutely no idea how to fill it. When inspiration comes, it can come at the most inconvenient moments; often when I'm in the middle of something that can't wait. Many times, inspiration hits just after I've gone to bed; in those few minutes before I'm fully asleep. If I don't get up and write down what I'm hearing, I know it will be lost. Sometimes, I have an inspiration when I'm driving down the highway and even if I stop, I have nothing to write on; so again, by the time I get to somewhere I can write, the inspiration has disappeared. Inspiration of this kind is a fleeting thing; it comes very quickly and leaves the same way. Sometimes when I'm writing, the thoughts come so quickly I am just scribbling to keep up with them. Those are the times I know the thoughts are not my own; mine are slower and more measured.

I once tried to skip the step of writing with my favorite pen on paper, as I sit in my comfortable recliner, but that seems to seriously interfere with the creative process. I recently discovered I like writing on scratch copy paper much better than the spiral notebooks I started with. The pen flows more smoothly and I can write longer without my hand cramping.

When I began writing I was documenting things that were happening after my son passed. The spiral notebooks helped to compartmentalize what I was writing. I had several journals going at the same time. They were color coded. The red ones were always my prayer journal, blue were personal reflections etc.

If I try to begin writing a book by selecting the title first, I soon discover that what I'm being inspired to write doesn't fit with that title. So far, the title comes to me somewhere in the middle of writing the chapters. I give each book a working title, but I do that knowing it will almost certainly change before the book is finished. You may be wondering what the value of explaining my writing process to you is; don't think I haven't wondered about that too! What comes to me is this: I often encourage people who are grieving, to begin writing in a journal. Most people think writing is much too hard for them. Perhaps sharing the process will make it easier for others to begin to document their feelings. It has been such a therapeutic exercise for me and I really think so many others could benefit from keeping a journal. You never have to share what you've written unless you feel compelled to do so.

When I began to write my thoughts about and to document the events surrounding the murder of my son, I had no intention of ever sharing it with anyone other than my immediate family. It was meant as a record of those events that my grandchildren might one day read and understand what happened when they were deep in grief for their father and walking through time in a daze; unaware of many of the things going on around them. I felt like they would have a lot of questions and perhaps, I wouldn't be here to answer them or my memory would fail. I originally believed I would create the record of that time and then never read it or think about those painful things again. I never intended for it to become a book. It was only after the Holy Spirit convinced me the story of our loss might help someone else find their way out of the darkness of grief, that I began to consider publishing those thoughts and memories. I also began to think of it as a possible help to those who knew someone who was deep in grief and that it might give them some insight to what that person was experiencing.

God and I had a conversation about my hesitation to publish the book. I told Him if it would help someone else, I would feel it was worth whatever amount of criticism it drew from those who wouldn't accept the truth of my experiences.

To my surprise, when I began to accept opportunities to tell my story to various groups, I received only their support and encouragement. Many people have trusted me with their own story of grief and unexplained spiritual happenings. I am blessed and grateful for the trust my story inspired in those people. I told God if the book would help just one person, I was willing to share it; it has helped many people so far and my greatest wish is that it will continue to circulate and touch as many others as possible.

It is not my intention to interfere with or try to change anyone else's spiritual or religious beliefs. I am not promoting or representing any organized church etc. I am just relating my personal experiences and the Truths I have found on my own journey. I believe there are many paths that lead to the same place. I also believe not all of the information about these things is widely known; no one has the whole picture and no one in this world is 100% right or wrong. The growth of your spirit is an individual journey and it doesn't happen in the same way for everyone. I only know it is important that it happen. It is important to seek this kind of growth, because you rarely find things you aren't looking to find.

4

ROSE COLORED GLASSES

My first thought was to begin this chapter by observing that, as a human being, I have a lot of good qualities and a few negative qualities (faults), but then it occurred to me, that human beings really have no qualities; it is the spirit within each person that bears qualities both good and bad. For nearly four years, I have been engaged in what could be called a "life review". I am searching the past to find meaning in my life. This process is very much like sorting through old boxes of photographs or scrapbooks. In case you are wondering; yes, I have found a great deal of meaning in my search.

As I have revisited the path my life has taken, I have seen many things with a new and more forgiving perspective. I am not only more forgiving of myself; I am much more forgiving of those I formerly found it so hard to forgive. Nothing that occurred in the past has changed in any way, but I am looking at the past with a changed heart and that makes a tremendous difference. I have written in previous books about my inability to forgive and how that was suddenly changed when the Holy Spirit led me to forgiveness of the man who took Ethan's life. In offering that forgiveness, I finally learned how to forgive myself for my own failures and that led to forgiveness of many others.

Whenever I come across something or someone in the past in need of forgiveness, I think to myself: you were able to forgive Shannon for taking your child's life; forgiving anything else should be easy and I find that it is. The unforgiving part of myself was like a huge stone wall; it seemed impenetrable and it was something I was afraid to allow to be destroyed. Fear can hold us back in so many ways, until we realize it is a trap. In the instant I allowed myself to forgive the murder of my son, that wall I believed was protecting me, came crashing down and I realized freedom had been held prisoner behind it.

I had found the freedom to live without bitterness or hatred and in doing so, found a new and easier path to walk on. I can now live my life unafraid of life's slings and arrows; they will still come, but I know I won't be handling them alone and I know how to see them with a forgiving heart. I try to move forward, with courage and hope.

When you understand that every human being is building some kind of wall of protection, you see them as being as vulnerable as you are and you recognize where the negativity you see in them is coming from. You begin to see them as another spirit, trying to navigate life in a strange and often hostile world. None of us will ever be 100% successful in viewing life here spiritually, but if we are willing to try, we will be blessed by the effort.

The song," Rose-colored Glasses", is about someone who loves another person so deeply, they are willing to look beyond their faults and see only the good in them. People often believe that viewing life through rose-colored glasses means you're choosing not to see reality and setting yourself up to be taken advantage of. I no longer see it that way; I believe looking through rose-colored glasses, is like seeing only through the filter of love and disregarding everything else. I think it's the way God sees us and loves us in spite of our faults.

In my study of "near death experiences", I've discovered nearly everyone who speaks of their experience with it, mentions a "life-review", but they aren't talking about "being judged", they are reviewing their own lives and seeing the mistakes they made and forgiving themselves. Does this mean there is no Divine judgement? I can't say there isn't, but I think God may be more interested in reconciliation than punishment of some kind.

5

DO YOU HEAR WHAT I HEAR?

So much of life on earth is perception and we don't all perceive things the same way. It's often said: Some people can't see the forest for the trees! Eyewitnesses often have very different perceptions of the exact same event.

So, what do being able to see clearly (perceiving) and the title of this chapter have to do with each other? Our earthly or human senses are very closely interactive. They work best when more than one of our five senses is active at the same time. For instance, if you have a bad cold and your nose is stuffy, it is almost impossible to taste your food. If your ears are covered and someone speaks to you, it is much harder to discern what they said using only your eyes. Our earthly senses are also closely tied to our spiritual senses. Our spirit perceives things more clearly when our heart and mind work together to process and understand the guidance we are receiving. When you hear spiritually, there is rarely an audible sound; you aren't using your human sense of hearing and it doesn't involve sound waves causing your ear drums to vibrate, as happens with your human auditory system. Many times, with spiritual perception someone will say: "I just know it; I don't know how I know, but I just do!" This "knowing" may show up as a thought that pops into your mind that you realize hasn't come from your brain. Most of us believe our thoughts originate solely in our brain and in the human sense, that's accurate to a degree. Your brain is a "processor" that is fed information from every other part of your body. It also receives information from everything around you. It perceives when your body is hot or cold, wet or dry, healthy or ailing etc.

For my purposes here, let me suggest to you that your brain and your mind are two different things. I'm not making any scientific statement here; it's just easier in this instance to see them as separate. I also want you to think of your mind as something without form and I want you to think of your heart the same way. We are not talking about the organ that beats in your chest and sustains your life. The heart we speak of here is without form, but very much in existence. Together your mind and heart are a channel of spiritual communication. I believe this is truly where our emotions live and where our conscience and consciousness exist.

This is the part of us that the Holy Spirit communicates with; for many people it is a one-way communication. It's like never answering your phone. Seeing and hearing spiritual communication doesn't take practice as much as it requires awareness and focus. It doesn't require the use of your eyes or your ears; instead it requires your mind and heart acting in tandem (together).

Often when people perceive some thought they can't identify as coming from their brain; they become frightened or wonder if they're "hearing voices that they shouldn't be hearing and are losing their sanity, so they resist acknowledging the voice they heard.

The thoughts I'm speaking of here are "spiritual thoughts"; a spiritual thought can't contain any negativity. For instance, if you are hearing a voice that relays thoughts of harming someone else or yourself, those are not spiritual thoughts. Those are dangerous thoughts and you need to see a professional immediately. Spiritual thoughts come from God, through His Holy Spirit, and God is love and incapable of negative or harmful thought or communication.

Spiritual thoughts can take you deeper than you ever knew it was possible to go. Thinking spiritually is such a freeing experience and produces serenity and peace in your soul. Spiritual thoughts often reveal a path to follow on your human pilgrimage through life. They reassure you that you are not, nor have you ever been truly alone. They do not condemn, but accept you as the perfect creation of God. Spiritual thinking allows you to hear the "still, small voice" of God; human thinking can't produce such wonderous results. Human thinking is often very negative and damaging to your spirit.

Many times, there is a disconnect between the thinking of our mind and the yearning of our heart; bringing them together creates a balance we badly need in our human lives and opens the channel to spiritual communication. When we pray, we are speaking to God; when we allow our heart and mind to connect, we can hear God speaking to us through the Holy Spirit. It is the most direct way humans have of communicating with Him.

Before Jesus came, God spoke only to and through His prophets; never to individual human beings; at least no communications of this kind are recorded in the Old Testament, according to Biblical scholars. Following Jesus death, the Holy Spirit was sent to us, just as Jesus promised in John 16:7: *"But, I say the truth to you. It is profitable for you that I go away; for if I go not away, the Comforter will not come unto you; but if I go, I will send Him to you."* We have the responsibility of opening the channel of communication; in order to hear Him speak to us. The thought of speaking so directly to God is frightening to a lot of people. Most of us wouldn't think of going years without speaking to our earthly father; God is our "Father in Heaven", as well as all of the other titles that describe Him as all- knowing and all powerful. We have been taught to actually "fear" Him, when what He really desires is our love and companionship. Someone you fear can never be considered a companion. He wants to hear what you have to say: He's a very good listener and He invented patience so you can talk as long as you want to.

"He who has ears, let him hear"
Matthew 13:9

6

HERE, THERE AND EVERYWHERE

*P*eople often ask: Where is God? Where is God in times of tragedy, pain, illness or death? Many people believe there is no definitive answer to these questions and anyone who thinks they have the answer is just guessing.

I don't presume to have all of the answers, but I know where God is not. He isn't sitting on a throne that's floating on a cloud, or somewhere out there beyond the farthest reaches of the universe. He doesn't reside only in churches and I don't believe He's giving demerits to those of us who don't think it's necessary to attend church and spread coronavirus to our friends and neighbors. In the midst of this health crisis, it's dangerous to believe that God will only meet with us inside a church and that if we don't do that, we will have failed a test of our faith. Many people sit in churches every Sunday for a lifetime and never truly commune with God; He is there, but they can't hear His voice.

When I was 12 years old and went through the baptism of immersion, because my parents decided it was the right thing to do and the right time to do it; I knew I was supposed to feel something, but I didn't. I did all of the things we are told to do as faithful believers; but I still felt nothing. I didn't feel it, or see it or hear it, until I lost my son when I was 64 years old.

For the first time God's word became clearly understandable and applicable in my life. God's word truly became *"a lamp unto my feet and a light unto my path"*. *(Psalm 119:105)*

For the first time I realized what it meant to have Jesus living in my heart, soul and mind. I understood what a life-changing event it was to receive Jesus' peace and to feel His calming presence every day, in spite of the devastating loss I had suffered.

God is here; in my heart. God is there; whenever I need Him or where ever I go. God is every where I look; in nature, in the beautiful sunrise and sunset, in the great expanse of the blue sky, in the rainbow, in the Spring, in the dark of night, in the deepest sorrow and the greatest joy.

God lives inside me, He walks beside me, He shares my pain and my weakness. He makes me more than I am and all I will ever be.

Praise His Holy Name!

7

LIKE A ROCK/THE WEIGHT

I am amazed as I look back at my life, at the seemingly mundane things that inspire me to write. This chapter is about a rock; that's not something I ever thought I'd be writing about. It is a rock I grew up with and about which I can recall many moments in time.

"The Rock", was in the backyard of the home I grew up in on Pine St.; it was a huge piece of concrete and not technically a rock. We were told by someone who had lived in the neighborhood for many years, the rock had been at the entrance of an old barn that had long since been demolished. The rock was rectangular in shape and about 6 ft. long, close to 3ft. wide and about 2-1/2 ft. high; it was a very big rock! It was more than a rock to me; it was a location.

It was a place to go to be alone and think my own thoughts. It was shaded most of the day by a mulberry tree, which also provided some privacy. It was a place I would often go to if I was mad or hurt, or pouting about something. I remember lying on the rock reading my favorite library book, *"Island of the Blue Dolphins"*. I read that book about 30 times; not always while lying on the rock. I also remember lying on my back on the rock and looking up at a million stars in the summer night sky. I can still remember the sound of the crickets and locusts as they sang their night time songs.

Sometimes, we would meet up at the rock and plan our adventures for the day, with the other neighborhood kids. Sometimes, our plans involved playing on or around it. I remember pretending it was Plymouth Rock and we were the newly arrived pilgrims. One of my strongest childhood memories of the rock was about a day we were playing calvary and Indians with some girls from the across the street. My brother got a new bow and some metal tipped arrows for Christmas and he hid behind the rock with the bow and an arrow to fight the calvary that was attacking the Indian village. He raised up from behind the rock at exactly the same time our friend Judy raised up on the other side and he let the arrow fly. Luckily, it only grazed her forehead. It was just an accident, but the use of the bow and arrows was much more restricted by the Chief in Charge, our mother.

During the period of my life after getting a divorce, my two young sons and I moved back to the house I grew up in on Pine St. My parents vacated it when they moved to another nearby town and I rented it from them for a few years. My kids often played on the rock too and I'm sure they have their own stories to tell. My most vivid memory of that time was when my oldest son Brett, had his seventh birthday. Tom and I were married by then and we gave Brett a shiny, new blue bicycle for his birthday. About two days later he left it out by the big rock overnight. When he went to get it the next morning, it wasn't where he'd left it. We hunted for awhile before we found it on the back side of the rock, missing both wheels and the seat. He was heartbroken. We recognized the shiny wheels and distinctive seat, on the old bicycle of a boy who lived a few blocks away. We said nothing about it and just bought Brett another bicycle.

These are all just memories of days gone by. These days, Jesus is my "Rock", and is helping me move forward and create many more happy memories.

No one goes through life without troubles; some people seem to have more than their share. Most earthly troubles come and go; they burden us for a time and then are resolved in some manner or we move on and they become irrelevant.

In Matthew 11:28 Jesus said: "Come to me, all of you who are weary and carry heavy burdens, and I will give you rest." He was speaking of spiritual and emotional burdens that weigh down your spirit and rob you of the peace Jesus wants you to live with.

People live with all kinds of burdens; the burden of low self-esteem or the inability to meet expectations of others; the burden of serious or limiting illness; the burden of disability or deformity, anxiety, or PTSD. It would be impossible to name every burden human beings could have to bear.

The burden many of us bear is the loss of a precious child and we will carry this burden for the rest of our time on Earth. It is like carrying a 20lb. rock with you everywhere you go. You can't lay it aside; you just have to carry it. You feel its weight every day; no matter what you are doing. There are days when it feels like an 80lb. rock; those are the days you are really struggling with your loss.

When you rest your burdens on Jesus, as He invites us to do, He doesn't promise to make it all go away. What He does is help you carry what is yours to bear. You will still feel the weight, but it doesn't overwhelm you and you know you are never alone with it. You are able to live, laugh and love, in spite of the weight you carry. Jesus doesn't expect you not to continue to feel the pain of your loss; or not to shed tears on those tough days that pop up out of nowhere. He never loses patience with you when you are struggling to regain your balance. He admires your ability to love so deeply and He has no expectation that you will just get over it someday. He never thinks you are wallowing in self-pity. He feels your pain and He helps you bear it every day. Jesus is love and compassion; He can't be otherwise. There is no need for you to carry the weight of grief alone; He is waiting for you to call to Him.

"Let not your heart be troubled"
John 14:1

8

PRETTY BLUE EYES

My mother used to introduce my little sister as "our blue-eyed baby girl". My eyes were brown and since I was never introduced as "our brown-eyed baby girl", I decided having brown eyes must be an inferior trait. It was one of many imagined slights that I took to my young heart and as the years passed, I began to number each one and store it away. By the time I was about 10 I had developed a full-blown inferiority complex; I have never clearly understood why.

I believe it has something to do with birth order. I was the middle child for about 6-1/2yrs. and I felt insignificant. I had an older brother, who was the only male child as well as the firstborn and I had a younger sister, Jeanne, who by all accounts was a sweet natured and pretty little girl. My youngest sister wasn't born until I was 10 and that didn't really change my position in my family much, except to create more responsibility for me as the oldest sister. Jeanne got a lot of attention from everyone, our parents, the neighbors, my parent's friends etc. People always bought her things or gave her gifts and sometimes they would ask if she could stay with them overnight. Nobody ever did those things in my case. It wasn't really Jeanne's fault, but I began to bitterly resent her because of it. She was pretty and I was ordinary; she was sweet and happy and I was shy and moody. As she got older, we began to be at odds most of the time. We were not close all of the years we lived at home with our parents and after I married, she seemed closer to my husband and children than to me. I don't think she understood where my rejection of her came from, but I know she felt it. She was someone I loved, but I couldn't have said at that time that I liked her and I imagine she felt the same way. Anyone who has known us for the past 30 years would find it hard to believe we haven't always been close.

One Summer, my grandmother wanted to go to Illinois to attend a reunion of her step family and my parents agreed to take her. Jeanne and I were both asked to go with them and we did. We arrived at Uncle Vernon's farm late in the afternoon, had a delicious meal and spent the rest of the evening visiting. When it was time to go to bed, we discovered Jeanne and I would have to share the upstairs bedroom, that had only a double bed.

We were pretty tired, so I expected we would both fall asleep quickly, but we started to talk and amazingly, we shared a whole lot of things about ourselves and our lives that neither of us knew about the other. Soon we were laughing and giggling and the old wire springs on the bed we were in were creaking loudly. This went on till the wee hours of the morning and with a minimum of sleep, we were called down to a huge breakfast much earlier than we had imagined. When we reached the bottom of the stairs, Grannie was sitting in a rocking chair, trying to wear a look of exasperation, and she said: *"I thought I was going to have to come up there and whip you girls so you'd stop that giggling and let me get some sleep."* I actually think she enjoyed the whole thing. Jeanne was 23 and I was 27 and at last, we had discovered each other.

We've had some ups and downs over the years since then and some of them were pretty serious. Then we shared the experience of caring for our mother in the last few weeks of her life. As we watched her life slipping away, we developed a much deeper empathy for each other. Since then, we have been touched by sorrow many times and each of those experiences takes us deeper into each other's soul. When I lost Ethan, she was there for me in a way no one but Ethan himself, could have been. For my part, there is no longer a place in my relationship with my sister, for petty squabbling. We have walked through the fire together and our spirits have been forged together in a closer bond than I ever knew was possible.

Me, Jeanne and our friend Debora

9

HEARTACHES BY THE NUMBER

*T*he first Mother's Day after losing my son, was one of the hardest days of my life. I have now lived through five Mother's Days since that loss. While they have gotten progressively less traumatic, I have the same thoughts every year. I believed that three children, was just the right number for me and now only two of them are here to share my life on this planet. One of the thoughts I had soon after losing Ethan was: *"What do I say when someone asks me how many children I have? Am I supposed to subtract one from that number and act as if Ethan never existed?"* That thought was and still is so offensive to me; I could never do that.

I make this point again now, because I still feel that people who haven't lived through the loss of a child can't ever fully realize the lasting impact it has on your life. The impact is felt in a million little ways beyond those that are obvious.

It is offensive to a bereaved parent when someone who means well, acts as if you can somehow be distracted from your loss by replacing who you lost with someone or something else. People are not interchangeable, they are not disposable; you can't replace one with another, nor can a human being be replaced with some "thing".

When people say to me: "*You still have two other children*", as though they think somehow, I've forgotten that fact; it is painfully clear to me that they don't or can't understand the magnitude of losing your child. You couldn't substitute one child for another, if you had 50 children. It's just not possible.

If I had been young enough to have another child, after Ethan's passing, it would have been just that, "another child". While that might be a distraction from your loss, it doesn't fill the hole in your heart, the space the lost child now occupies from another world. I feel Ethan's spirit, his love, every day of my life, from the place where he has gone and that is a great comfort to me, but it doesn't fill the void that only his "physical" presence could fill.

I love my other two sons just as much as I love Ethan. I love them as the unique individuals they are and for the special qualities they each possess. I love them for the things only they are capable of bringing to my life. My relationship with them is unique and couldn't be replaced by anyone else on earth or in heaven: and so it is with Ethan. My heart will continue to long for him until I can touch him again, in heaven.

When you lose someone, there are many days that are painful to you. The firsts you experience the next twelve months that follow the loss are extremely difficult to get through; the first birthday, Mother's Day or Father's Day, the anniversary of the date your loss occurred. Family holidays, wedding anniversaries; you can't keep from stopping to count how many of these occasions have passed since you were with the one you lost. You are reminded of how long it has been since you looked into their eyes, or felt their arms wrapped around you in a familiar gesture of love; how long it has been since you held their hand or heard them laugh.

God has blessed me with amazing comfort and

unexplainable peace in the 5 years since I lost my son, but He hasn't erased the pain of that loss; He just makes it bearable. He never said we wouldn't suffer pain in this world. He just said He would be with us when our hearts are broken and our tears are falling. He has created for me, a way to live with joy and peace every day, but not every moment. I wouldn't have it any other way. I am grateful that I can have those moments to remember Ethan with love and gratitude for the life he had and shared with us. Love and pain are co-mingled now; my love is real and so is my pain and both are meant to be experienced.

10

WRECK OF THE EDMUND FITZGERALD

*T*his chapter title is a song about an actual shipping disaster that occurred on Lake Superior. A freighter carrying many tons of iron ore was caught in one of the sudden storms that often occur on the big lake and it sank with twenty-nine souls on board. There is a line in the song that asks a question people frequently ask when disaster strikes: Where is God when unspeakable tragedy occurs? Does He orchestrate such horrific events and the loss of life they bring? Does He just look the other way? Does He not care?

People often believe God is false, if they pray for someone's life to be spared and it doesn't happen as they wished. It is common for people to blame God for loss of life in any situation where it occurs. These are emotional reactions to highly emotional circumstances. Human beings seem to have a need to assess blame and God usually receives the blame when something painful happens.

When I lost my son, it never occurred to me to blame God. Some would argue that if God was not the direct cause, He still could have intervened in some way and prevented Ethan's life from being taken. Surely, we all realize it isn't God's plan that none of us will die. I guess in order to have that realization, you first have to know and accept that there is a plan; there is a plan for each individual life and there is a plan for all of our lives collectively. Do I wish God had intervened and saved Ethan's life? Of course, I do, but I also accept that it wasn't His plan to do so. I believe God's plan for Ethan's life was prematurely interrupted, by the will of the man who took it. The fact that God didn't intervene in that moment, may have saved Ethan many years of extreme pain and disability, had he lived with such severe injuries. Our bodies are not designed to function beyond a certain level of destruction. The Bible says, God's thoughts are not our thoughts and His purposes are not our purposes. God's thoughts are much higher than ours and we can't begin to understand them. We have to learn to trust God completely, even when we don't like what happens or understand why it happened. Many people say they believe in God, but when tragedy occurs, do they really trust Him.

The use of the word "fear" in the Bible, leads to a lot of misunderstanding. Perhaps I should say, it isn't that the word is used; it's that our understanding of it now, is so different than it was when the Bible was written. If you look up the definition of the word fear, most often the last entry says something like this: (Archaic) meaning very old and unused); regard (God) with reverence and awe. That sounds a lot different than fear as we know it today.

It is easy for people to believe God is responsible for every accident or illness or tragedy that occurs. Why is it so hard to believe He loves each of us and has no plan to harm us? Jeremiah 29:11 says: *"For I know the plans I have for you; plans to prosper you and not to harm you: plans to give you hope and a future."* God doesn't cause our pain and suffering. He doesn't choose to make one person sick and another die tragically before their time. God is there to help us pick up the pieces of our lives and try to find a way to go on living. He doesn't play games with our lives. We belong to Him and He wants our lives to be wonderful. When you begin to understand that your spirit can't die or be destroyed, death takes on a different meaning; it loses its power over us. We survive death as spirit for eternity.

I can't even imagine how I would have survived the horror and heartbreak of losing Ethan, without the strength, courage, hope and peace God supplied to me.

God would indeed have to be a treacherous monster to cause your heart to shatter and then try to convince you He only wanted to help you heal it; that makes no sense and nothing exists that substantiates such thinking.

Life in this world is full of risk and danger; things happen to people we love and we are left heartbroken and in the throes of grief. God is our refuge, not our tormentor; God is love and He cannot be otherwise.

11

SMALL TOWN

*T*he current population of the world is estimated to be 8.7 billion people. Even those of us who live longest will never meet even a fraction of the number of spirits existing here on Earth at any given time.

The title of this chapter is a song by John Mellencamp, about the small Indiana town he grew up in. Like most teenagers he felt somewhat stifled there; it was only when he became an adult that he realized that small town had become an integral part of who he was.

A few years ago, if you had asked me about my hometown, I would have said I grew up in Peabody, Ks., population around 1200 at that point in time. My spiritual journey has revealed that "my town" is really composed of every spirit whose life path has intersected with mine. That is so, no matter how brief or lengthy a period of time that convergence may have lasted.

Time has taught me how necessary each of these interactions was to the unfolding of my life story; each furthers our personal narrative in some way, even if we don't recognize or understand it. I have learned that my circle, "my town", is much larger than the place I called home for so many years.

Like most people I am extremely close to my family and

having lost a son who was not only a precious child, but also a kindred spirit, my family has become even more precious; they are the most special of all of the spirits given to me to share a life with.

There is another group of people that I am extremely fond of and who hold a place of great importance in my life; my friends. I will soon be 69 years old and over the span of those years, I was fortunate to have been blessed with several "best" friends. I know there are people out there who claim to have never shared a relationship like that; keep looking and someday that special friend will cross paths with you, because it is destined for you to meet. When you meet this person, you will most likely feel an instant bond that makes it seem as if you have met before, or have known each other in another life and time.

Recently, I have been blessed to rekindle one of my oldest friendships. Karen and I grew up in the same neighborhood; I lived on Pine St. and she lived on Spruce St., one block over from my house. No one introduced us, we just met one day at a place everyone in the neighborhood called the "Monkey Bars". It was really just a small concrete bridge that helped you cross a deep ditch and there were bars to hold onto as you crossed. All of the kids played on the bars, like they were put there for our gymnastic exploits. We became close friends and maintained our relationship until I married shortly before I graduated from high school. Karen was the maid of honor at my wedding, but soon afterward, we had a falling out. I have to say it was mostly my fault and had I been a bit more mature and understanding of her feelings, it would never have happened.

Sadly, one of the things that brought us back together was that she too, had lost a son. That kind of loss puts everything in your life into a completely different perspective. It creates a very strong bond, because it's so hard to find people who truly understand how such a loss feels and how it changes you and impacts your life forever.

It is also a sad fact that most of the best friends I've had has each lost a child. The percentage of parents overall who have lost a child is around 3.4. Within my circle of closest friends, which includes 10 people, 7 of 10 have lost a child. That percentage really blew my mind when it occurred to me. There are many more friends and acquaintances who have also lost children; I know several people who have lost more than one child. I really have no plausible explanation for this many losses in so small a group of people, but I can definitely say I have had lots of experience with this type of loss. I can't say what all of this means, except that I know it's somehow very important. Knowing so many people who have endured such a loss, is one of the things that inspires me to write about my own experience. All of these people, as well as the strangers I meet when I speak publicly, are part of my town.

There is a famous play, written by Thornton Wilder, that is titled "Our Town". It is about life and death; when I visit the cemetery where my son's earthly body is resting, the thoughts of all of those people there who passed into my life and then out again flood my mind. I am somewhat surprised at the fondness that is evoked when I pass through the cemetery and recognize so many of the names of those interred there. I used to think of most of these people as just casual acquaintances, who had little impact on my life; now I realize they too are inhabitants of my town. They somehow belong to me and I to them.

As I write this chapter, I am reminded of one of the inhabitants of Prairie Lawn Cemetery. Her name was Carrie

Dietrich and she lived in my neighborhood. She seemed very, very old and she was about as big around as the handle of a broom. She was bent over at the waist and had a large hump on her back; which I now know was caused by osteoporosis. She was a friend of my Aunt Anna's and my uncle would frequently take her to town so she could buy groceries for herself and the brother who lived with her. Carrie was a very cranky lady and I tried my best to avoid her because she made me uncomfortable. Children know when adults don't like them.

When I turned seven, I got a new blue bicycle for Christmas. I waited anxiously for Spring to arrive, so I could learn to ride it. I had just become proficient enough to have the training wheels removed, when something awful occurred. I was riding my bicycle down the dirt street next to our home, when along came Carrie walking with her cane. She was on her way to visit Mrs. Taylor, who lived just across the street from my house. It was a very windy day; Carrie looked up and saw me coming on my bicycle, still about 20 ft. from her and decided I was aiming to hit her. I had no such intention! She shrieked and threw her arms up over her head, just as a huge gust of wind caught her and lifted her off the ground and then dropped her several feet away. I was so terrified of this little lady waving her cane and shrieking like a banshee, that I dropped my bike in the street and ran into my house and hid in the bedroom. A few minutes later, one of the neighbors came to the door to tell my mother, Carrie was telling anyone who would listen that I had hit her with my bicycle, on purpose. I was horrified; I refused to even go out to play for several days. Carrie wasn't seriously injured, just frightened and angry, but she was never convinced that I didn't hit her and that I meant to.

Throughout my life review, I have come across incidents such as this where a misunderstanding led to suspicion or hard feelings and I often feel the need to try to resolve these things wherever possible. Carrie has been gone for many years, but it has just occurred to me that I should some day leave a rose at her grave, to make it up to her for picking bachelor's buttons from her yard, many years ago, but not for hitting her with my bicycle; because that never happened!

The terrible loss of life all across the world from the coronavirus pandemic, shows me that all are part of my town; all are important to my life and I have an innate fondness for each spirit living in this world; even those I find it hard to like.

At times, when I was growing up in my small hometown, the world seemed so large and my town so small, but I've learned the world is so much smaller than I knew and my town is infinitely larger than I could ever have imagined.

12

AMONG MY SOUVENIRS

A well-known TV personality, whose talent is home décor, recently stated on one of the online forums, that there is one decorating style we should all hope never returns: It was my house she was talking about.

Perhaps, my decorating style isn't really a recognized decorating philosophy; but it's me. I call It "Grandma's House". It is a blend of eclectic and nostalgic and not a lot different than what is called "Cottage Style".

In actual fact, I'm not terribly concerned that a woman I don't know and will never meet, doesn't like my decorating efforts. I don't do it to make other people happy, or comfortable.

My home is my sanctuary; a place of refuge. I choose colors that soothe and relax me; I never consider what the experts say is the current color of the year. I choose furniture that is comfortable and suits my needs. At least 95% of what I own is antique and not necessarily the same time period. I like antiques because of the way they look and the quality craftsmanship that produced them. The fact that they have a history makes me feel grounded in some inexplicable way. A number of the pieces I own are family heirlooms;

they belonged to people we loved who are no longer with us. Anything that reminds me of someone I love or who loves me, gives me comfort.

There is a table in my kitchen, that has been in my family since the early 1930's; four generations of my family have shared a meal or learned to play cards or shared stories or worries at that table. It has served many Thanksgiving Dinners in it's time.

It isn't a beautiful table, but to me it is priceless. It came to me after my Aunt Anna passed and it was in bad shape. My husband repaired it and removed the old finish that had turned nearly black. When he was refinishing the table, we found that it had the mark of a flat iron burned into the top. My husband asked if I wanted him to try to remove it; I said, *"No, leave it there, Anna put it there and it's almost like an autograph".* Over the years the table has been in our possession, the burn mark has slowly disappeared, but I will always remember it and the woman who put it there.

When Anna passed away; I grieved her loss for several years. During that time, I crocheted a round tablecloth to use on her table, which at that time sat in my dining room. It took me 3 years to finish the tablecloth and when it was done, my time of grieving came to an end. Someone once offered me a large amount of money for that tablecloth and at that time I could really have used the money, but it is much too precious to reduce its value to any sum of money. It is one of my treasures, because it combines her love and my grief.

In the home I now live in, the tablecloth is on another very precious table. In early 2002, my sister and I were caring for our mother as she passed the final six weeks of her life. It was a devastating time for us, as we watched her grow weaker each day and it took a toll on all of us.

One day, about an hour after I arrived at Mother's to relieve Jeanne, who had been there all night, the phone rang; it was Tom and he wanted me to come home, because he said there was something I needed to see. I assumed it was some problem or other that had suddenly arisen. I was nearly exhausted from stress and lack of sleep and I told him I just couldn't handle one more negative thing. He just said *"You better come home."* At the time, we were living in a large Victorian home that had a foyer with a beautiful oak staircase and a parquet floor. The light fixture in that room hung very low and nearly everyone had to duck to keep from bashing their head. I looked quite awhile to find the perfect piece of furniture to put under the light fixture and would look appropriate.

The same year my mother was sick, the local furniture store donated a round game table to one of the local organizations, to raffle for a fundraiser. As soon as I saw the table, I knew it was perfect for the foyer, but you had to win it. I bought a couple of tickets, crossed my fingers and waited. They drew the winning ticket right before Christmas and, sadly it wasn't mine. Though disappointed, I decided to try one more time and I went to the furniture store to look for a matching table. I walked through their many showrooms and didn't see anything like it. I told myself I would have to look for something else later, my focus was really on losing my mother.

I hung up the phone at Mother's after talking to Tom and went home. I came through the back door into the kitchen and called his name. *"In here,"* he said. As I walked through the kitchen and into the dining room, I turned toward the foyer, he was leaning into the doorway. *"There's your table"* he said. There under the light fixture, was an identical table to the one sold in the raffle. I couldn't believe it. As always, he was more persistent than I was and he also went to the furniture store to look for another table, but he asked someone and discovered they had one more in storage.

My husband would do just about anything to make a bad situation better and though he knew there was nothing he could do to prevent what was happening to my mother, he wanted to make me smile by giving me the table I wanted. It now sits in the parlor of my new home, a smaller Victorian cottage and it's just as perfect under the light fixture as it had been in the bigger house.

I have learned over the years and through a number of sad losses, that "things" aren't really all that important and when my time comes to leave this world and be reunited with those I miss, I'll gladly leave all of my things behind. But, until that day comes, these things are like old friends, who wrap their arms around me whenever I need a hug and pause to think of the person they used to belong to. They are part of my sanctuary; I take care of them and in some inexplicable way they take care of me too.

Tablecloth I made in memory of Aunt Anna after she passed.

13

COBWEBS AND DUST

*W*hen I was a child, growing up on Pine St., there were several elderly ladies who lived in our neighborhood. Most of them were very nice and I would sometimes go to visit them. Usually, they would invite me to come in and occasionally, they would offer me a treat.

I was fascinated with each of these lady's homes and some of the things in them made a lasting impression on me. The home I live in now is very reminiscent of those I used to visit. They had lace curtains, crocheted doilies, pretty teacups, fancy throw pillows, etc. My house has all of these things too. It makes me feel warm and safe; it reminds me of good times and good people.

My house has something else in common with those elderly ladies' homes: dust! When I would visit them, I always wondered about the cobwebs and dust; I thought perhaps they just couldn't see well enough to notice them. Now, I realize it wasn't poor eyesight; it was the wisdom that comes with age. They had lived long enough to realize that dust wasn't the ultimate adversary. They had come to understand there are much more pleasant and important things to think about in life.

The dust isn't going to go anywhere, if you don't deal with it today, or tomorrow or even next week. I'm sure those ladies had spent as many years as I have fighting dust at every turn; dust always wins that battle. I'm sure you don't get points somewhere for having a dust free home; just as I'm sure you don't get demerits for a home that's sometimes dusty. I'm not advocating life in a filthy, disgusting home, just that there are many more important things to think about.

I became friends with a woman once, who had been a good friend of my mother's. She was older and wiser than I was and she told me one day when I mentioned that I had trouble getting all of the cleaning done, because my husband would frequently interrupt me to go sit in the yard swing with him, that there was nothing more important than that. She was right!

I was a cleaning lady for about 20 years, off and on, and I got really good at making things shine and eliminating all traces of dust, spots, finger prints, wrinkles and clutter. I got a lot of satisfaction from making someone's house look like a picture from a magazine; like it was frozen in time, but neither time nor hell actually freeze over and when I returned the next week, all of my hard work had been undone. People lived in those houses; I live in mine also, that's what it's meant for. It serves me and I do not have to be a slave to it.

My home is my sanctuary, with or without dust. It is filled with all kinds of old-fashioned things that other people loathe; that's okay, they don't live here.

Recently, a woman who runs a business that conducts estate sales, wrote an open letter to people like me. She said a lot of things, many of which, I could take exception to if I wanted to expend the energy; which I don't. She said some things I was already pretty sure were true; namely this: *"Wake up, people!*

Your children don't want to have to live with any of your old junk!
They don't want your china, or Grandma's either. They don't want
your silver tea set, or your teacup collection, or crystal glassware.
They don't want your old quilts or the antique four-poster bed they fit
on! So, get over it!!"

My father often said, he'd never seen a hearse pulling a U
Haul trailer; you can't take it with you. I recently heard Denzel
Washington elaborate on that statement and he added: *"The*
Egyptians tried that and all they got was robbed!" I have no plans
to take anything with me, but I also have no plans to divest
myself of any of my treasures before I go. They will be here to
comfort me as long as I'm here and when I'm gone, my family
can do as they wish with them.

I also have no wish to spend my last days, hours, and
minutes dusting and mopping floors. I want to be writing or
enjoying my flowers and listening to the birds sing. I want to
see my grandchildren happy in meaningful lives and I want
them to remember me as someone who tried to teach them
what life was really about. I have no wish to be remembered as
a great duster!

14

FOR WHOM THE BELL TOLLS

*T*his title has had several incarnations; it is a song I love by the Bee Gees; it is a novel by Ernest Hemingway, published in 1940; but it began as a meditation written by John Donne in 1624 and published within *"Devotions Upon Emergent Occasions"*. It is often presented in poetic form and I read it in English Literature, while in high school; it made a lasting impression on me. The premise of the prose/slash poem is that anyone's death affects all of us. Long ago it was the custom in many places to announce a death by ringing the church bells. In the town I grew up in, there was a message board that announced the death of and services for those who passed. How many times have you asked someone; who died? I've done it hundreds of times in my own life.

My interpretation of Donne's writing here is that it on one hand speaks to the subject of empathy. Empathy is sort of the first cousin of compassion; these are both considered desirable qualities in emotionally balanced human beings. To be devoid of empathy means you are unable to place yourself in the position of someone who is sad, depressed, grief stricken, distraught, etc. In other words, you are unable to feel the pain someone else is experiencing and understand it in a way that allows you to feel sympathy for them and offer emotional support.

Not everyone who lacks empathy is seriously mentally ill, but many people devoid of empathetic tendencies have become serial killers, who lack the capacity to feel the pain they inflict on their victims. Lacking empathy is to various degrees a serious emotional imbalance that contributes to an inability to really connect with others and the world in general.; of itself it isn't considered a mental illness, but it can be a characteristic of several mental conditions, such as, sociopathy, psychopathy and narcissism.
Some psychologists say that if a child has not developed empathy by the time they are 6yrs. old, it is likely they never will; however it is possible with concerted effort to develop empathy later in life. In order to do that, one would need to consider it a desirable quality; many people today consider it a sign of weakness. For example; in business it is considered a valuable tool to know what your competitor is thinking, but knowing or focusing on how he/she feels, lessens your ability to act with firmness or even ruthlessness when it's deemed necessary.

Going back to the language in "For Whom The Bell Tolls", it's other important theme is "one of "connection". It speaks to the connection of all human beings to each other; the "brotherhood of man". The importance of this brotherhood, has been seriously devalued in our society at present; one has to wonder if it will ever be restored. I sincerely hope it will be; it's one of the things that makes us behave more humanely toward each other emotionally, physically and very importantly, spiritually.

We live in a world where so much of our attention is focused on personal happiness and well-being; with little thought given to the well-being of others. Our attitude seems to be; *"Let them take care of themselves, it's nothing to me."*

In another chapter of this book, I spoke about losing some of my classmates. I mentioned a boy named Randy; because Randy passed in November of the year we graduated, many of our classmates had left for college and could not attend his service. I felt it was appropriate to send flowers from our class, even though there was no class fund at that time to pay for such things. I went to the homes of some of my classmates and asked if their parents would be willing to donate money for flowers for a classmate of their son or daughter. Most parents were happy to do so and thanked me for making the effort. I have never forgotten the one parent who at first refused and then very grudgingly gave me about 80 cents, while telling me not to expect her to do it in the future.

I am the kind of person who would donate money for funeral flowers for a total stranger, if someone asked me to do that. Why would I? Because I believe very strongly in the brotherhood of man. Before you think it, and I know someone will; Yes, I know that term is probably not "politically correct". It's not in its proper context a sexist term; it means all of us and I think most of us know that. Many today would say it's improper because it sounds as if it excludes women; that completely misses the material point.

Returning to the story of Randy, I collected enough money to buy a nice flower arrangement and the few of my classmates who attended his service, were happy I had done so. I continued to fill that role for the next 45 years. After my son's passing, I moved from my hometown and tried to give the responsibility to someone else; I couldn't find anyone who was willing, so I took the little bit of money let in the class account and donated it to the high school alumni association.

While I was in English Literature reading John Donne's work, I read a commentary that likened his sentiments to a book losing its pages one by one; as each page is lost the book begins to lose its value and is diminished. As with a book, humanity loses something as each human being leaves the earth, because we are all part of the whole of Creation and each brings something unique to this world. It matters that we take the time to honor those who leave us and acknowledge that all are diminished with each departure.

Funerals are about the departed, but they are for those who remain in the world. I have never attended a funeral where I didn't learn something, I had previously not known about the person being remembered. Often it is something surprising or endearing or enlightening, as it may explain a lot about them, that helps me to understand the way they were in life.

I had a cousin who was deaf from the time he was about two years old. When I attended the service for him, I learned he had a huge record collection and if he turned the stereo up loud enough to put everyone else in the room on the floor, he could hear something and at least enjoy the vibrations the music created. I found that revelation fascinating, but I was a little bit sad when I realized how much we really don't know about each other. That inspired me to make an effort to get to know as many of my cousins as I could in a much more personal way. I knew them all of my life, but I never really knew them. Getting to know them better has been a wonderful experience and I hope they feel the same way I do.

I don't believe any of us are so important or busy that we can't take an hour or so to say a heartfelt goodbye to someone we knew in this life. When you have been on the receiving end of the condolences and emotional support of those who do, you never forget what those hugs and kind words did for your sad heart.

> *"Blessed be the God and Father of our Lord Jesus Christ, the Father of Mercies and the God of all comfort, who comforts us in all our tribulation, so that we may be able to comfort those who are in any trouble, with the comfort with which we ourselves are comforted by God."*
>
> *II Corinthians 1:3-5*

15

FAREWELL PARTY

I have discovered in the past few years that there are certain topics that most people avoid; one is death and the next in line is funerals. Even before we found ourselves caught up in the inevitable changes the coronavirus pandemic has forced on us, I had noticed some changes in the way many people were choosing to handle the loss of loved ones. To begin with, I used to own a small floral business, so I noticed a trend away from the custom of sending flowers as an expression of sympathy. Then I noticed that many people were opting for graveside services, memorial services or no service at all. Please don't think I'm presumptuous enough to think I have a right to tell others how to handle a situation as personal as this, as it pertains to their loved ones. It is what I see beneath the surface of these trends that I find disturbing. No one likes funerals; I think it's safe to make that statement, but I believe they serve a deeper purpose than a lot of people think. First, let me give you the usual reasons people give for opting out of traditional services; it's too expensive, flowers just wilt and die and again, too expensive. Then they might say; there's so little family left and all of his/her friends are gone etc. We don't have a home church and we don't know a minister or anyone willing to speak. He/she didn't like funerals and didn't wish to be seen. What's the point if they are going to be cremated anyway? I've heard all of these arguments and many more; but I think there are just as many reasons for taking the time and bearing reasonable expense in order to say a proper farewell, to those you love. People seem to really detest the word 'proper" these days, but I'm choosing to use it here anyhow.

When I write, I often look up definitions of words on my phone; usually I know what I would say the definition is, but I just want a different perspective. I use my phone, because I don't write my first drafts using a computer, most of us don't own or can't find a dictionary, or have perhaps decided it's only viable use is to hold a door open.

The definition of the word "funeral" says: a ceremony to honor and remember a deceased person". I was not surprised when I read the most commonly asked questions on this topic: What is the cheapest way to have a funeral? Is it rude not to go to a funeral? Can I wear jeans to a funeral? Then there were comments such as this: The funeral business is just a racket and I refuse to support such a waste of money!

It isn't the practicality of the decision that disturbs me, it's the insensitivity that seems to be growing around the subject of funerals. Instead of being held to honor and remember someone's life, that someone having been a human being and a creation of God, many people are only focused on disposal of remains; that seems pretty cold to me. Everyone was someone to somebody!

Attending a funeral is no one's idea of a great way to spend an hour or so, but it is now, and always has been a way to show respect for the person who is no longer here and to show love and compassion to a grieving family. How can things like this go out of fashion? Or is it just that people are more concerned with their time and money these days, than they used to be? I have attended countless funerals; most of us have. After they are over, I never wonder why I took the time to come. They have an intangible power; they make the majority of us feel a little better. They begin the actual healing process for the family who has just said goodbye to one they loved.

When my son's life was taken, I was in such a state of hysteria that I wondered how on earth I would make it through a large public funeral, but it never occurred to me not to have one. I knew there were so many people who knew and loved or respected Ethan, and they needed the opportunity to say their own goodbyes, but they also needed to see with their own eyes that what seemed impossible was actually so.

Ethan's service could not take place until 5 days after he passed; it was much longer than we would have waited in another circumstance and by that time he did not look as presentable as we would have wished. His passing was traumatic and it showed, but I wanted to give those who needed that closure the opportunity to say goodbye to him.

Years ago, when I was in the eighth grade, I had a teacher who had been a part of our community nearly all of her life. She and I didn't get along really well and that was almost entirely my fault. She had very strict rules of what she deemed acceptable behavior and I sometimes pushed the line too far. In spite of that, I did have a great deal of respect for her as a person.

As the young wife of a military pilot and the mother of two young sons, she had endured the loss of her husband in an aviation accident. She returned to our town and raised her sons alone. Many years later, she found someone she wanted to spend the remainder of her life with. A marriage ceremony was set to take place in another state and only a few close friends and relatives traveled there to witness her marriage. On the evening of the rehearsal, she suffered an aneurysm in her brain and passed away within hours. Our community was shocked and saddened by the news of her death. There was no funeral and no burial; she was cremated. For years it was so hard to believe she was really gone, because there was no place to go to leave flowers or see her name on a stone, as testimony that this unbelievable tragedy had occurred.

While I don't believe any of us owe it to the public to place their needs above our own at such a time, I do know it leaves something unfinished inside many people when there is no opportunity to say goodbye in a meaningful way. I guess that's really the important word in this chapter;" meaningfulness". Whatever happens in this regard, it should have meaning; if you love someone in life and would do anything for them, your treatment of them in death should reflect nothing less.

I have had to accept the fact that the world is constantly changing; I've never been good with change. Not all changes are bad, but neither does it make sense to change things that are meaningful into something cheap and meaningless. So far, at least, we have a choice as to how we will say goodbye to those we love and grieve for, but I wonder if it will continue to be so in the future.

16

ONLY THE GOOD DIE YOUNG

I believe there comes a point in nearly every life when you realize you've buried way too many young people. Do I believe that "only the good die young"? Of course not, but I believe many very good people live shorter lives than one would expect.

The burden of these losses began to weigh much heavier after I lost my son, but he was by far not the first young person I cared about who's casket I looked into and realized with sadness the potential that had been unfulfilled. Of course, Ethan was my child and there's no closer relationship you can have with another human being, but it's hard to lose anyone you care about.

When I was in high school a man came to speak to us about what the future might hold for my classmates and myself. He said statistics showed that five years after our graduation, we would probably have lost one or two of our classmates. He gave statistics for ten years, twenty years and fifty years. At fifty years, he predicted half of our class would be deceased.

The Peabody High School Class of 1969 had about forty-eight members. Our graduation date was in late May; in early November of that year, barely five months later, we lost our first classmate. His name was Randy; he died in a drag race. His death made us all feel vulnerable, shocked and saddened. We did pretty well for about twenty years after that; then we lost a woman named Patsy to leukemia. Patsy and I met the first day of kindergarten, we were girl scouts together and high school twirlers with the marching band. Patsy had a daughter, her only child, the same year my son Jeff was born. A couple of months after her death our children graduated together from the same high school Patsy and I graduated from twenty years earlier.

In the twenty years that have passed since then, we have lost several classmates to cancer, one in a car-train accident, one to ALS, one with a congenital heart condition and one from injuries related to a fall. None of these people reached seventy years old. Seventy seems pretty old to you until you're staring it in the face and it seems even younger when you think of someone not reaching that number of years.

Now we are living in the age of the coronavirus pandemic and death is all around us. As a young adult, I never thought I'd hear a more frightening word than cancer and then along came HIV. I couldn't imagine anything as bad as those two things and now here is a virus that can be contracted from people who don't know they're sick and don't appear to be sick; that is indeed a frightening thing. Coupled with the fact that it's nearly impossible to predict who will actually die from coronavirus or the extreme complications that often accompany it, the prospect is pretty unsettling.

A well-known media person recently commented that "dying is what people do". Yes, we all realize that, but preventable deaths are especially hard to accept. When you have been as close to death and dying as I have, you begin to shift your sorrow and grief to those who remain; those who mourn and whose hearts are forever broken by these losses. Because of my experiences and my spiritual beliefs, I realize that at least initially, everyone returns to the place they existed before being born into this world; beyond that I can't say with any certainty.

I think perhaps, some of you reading this are a bit hung up over the title of this chapter. We just can't help wondering why good people would die so young. I can't say I have the definitive answer to that question; maybe it can't be reduced to a single answer that fits all of these losses. The one thing I definitely know is that it has nothing to do with punishment, retribution, vengeance or sin. In the case of my son, who was murdered, the essence of my belief is: Ethan died because we all are given free-will by God and we decide how we will exercise that will in any given situation. The person who took Ethan's life made a choice to commit the most egregious act; the taking of another human life without just cause. Initially, I believed this couldn't have been how Ethan's life was meant to unfold, but I don't believe in coincidence, so now I am left with the fact that there must have been some pre-planned element to what happened. That is something I am sure I won't understand until I make my own transition to the place, we all initially arrive upon leaving this world.

I don't believe we are ever done growing and changing, even after we transcend. I believe there is much more to come for all of us and the choices we make in this life is a determining factor as to what our continuing story will be.

17

RING THEM BELLS

One day the call will come for each of us to return to our real home; the heavenly home we came from. Whether you believe that is a place beyond the sunset or simply another level of consciousness, you will return there. I believe we will all go there at least initially; beyond that I really can't say. Many people believe there are only two options; heaven or hell. I believe there are many levels of spiritual understanding (or heaven) and I believe God never decides He's finished with us. I think it's more like a never- ending cycle of spiritual development.

Many people believe there is an actual gate at the entrance to heaven; a pearly gate, and that St. Peter will be waiting there to grant or deny us permission to enter. I believe there is an entrance, but the gate is a metaphor. It is easier to picture a gate, than to say there is a point of access.

If there were an actual gate and St. Peter were the gatekeeper, he would be an apt choice for the position, but only if you believe it's possible for imperfect humans to enter into heaven. Peter was described as stubborn, disgruntled, often angry and not easily convinced. That description could describe many of us. If you believe Peter is the man for the job, then you have to believe people can change. You have to believe in redemption, forgiveness, unconditional love and that there is hope for the worst among us.

We are often taught that God abhors our imperfections and turns away from those who just can't seem to figure life out. It is our imperfections and our mistakes that gives God a place to work from. The key is that we have to recognize our mistakes and imperfections as being in need of change.

I have written several times about my own resistance to change, but I have come to recognize change as the key to growth, and spiritual growth is always a step forward. Spiritual growth gives us more strength, more courage, more hope, more joy; more of everything desirable.

Our lives here aren't meant to be just one problem after another. As each problem or dilemma is resolved, we gain something, but if we choose to focus only on the fact that a problem has presented itself and see it as just one more to add to a long list, we won't see it as an opportunity for growth.

When we approach each problem as a challenge to be worked through, and seek to understand its potential for positive personal growth, we turn something negative into an opportunity for gain, instead of just another loss. When this approach becomes a habit, we will have acquired a valuable tool with which to live life with more confidence, certainty and joy.

There is an old church hymn titled: "Count Your Many Blessings", to my knowledge there isn't one titled: "Count Your Problems" or "Count Your Mistakes". Many of us habitually keep a mental list of every little annoyance, every mistake, every problem, etc. that presents itself. That tendency causes us to live much of our lives overwhelmed with what seems, in its totality, to be an insurmountable mountain of troubles. It is far better to take one issue at a time, deal with it, find the meaning in it and move on to the next. The feeling of accomplishment that you get with having overcome even something insignificant, is as important as the imagined exhilaration of overcoming a mountain of woes.

Many of us live our lives with a self-defeating attitude which means we usually defeat ourselves before we've even begun to try to solve our problems. Then we allow these self-inflicted defeats to convince us that we are incapable and lack value or worthiness. Time after time of seeing ourselves this way, hides God's love and light behind our self-made darkness.

Behind those dark clouds, God's light still shines and we should devote all of our efforts to finding it. It is, after all, meant to shine on all of us. We are here in this world to experience and not all of our experiences will be pleasant; Jesus said: *"In this world you will have trouble. But, take heart! I have overcome the world"*. John 16:33

When I was a young woman, I often felt depressed. I realize now how I fed that depression, by keeping a running total of every little thing that hurt or upset me. I was nurturing all of those things, just as if I was feeding and watering a plant, and just like a plant the hurt and rejection continued to grow.

It was only when God gave me the courage and insight, I needed to break this cycle of self-inflicted damage, that I was able to slowly build a better life for myself and my children. When you are so far down in a pit, even one of your own making, you need a strong arm to pull you out. That arm is God's, even if it appears in the form of another human being. They are there because God sent them, even when they are unaware that they have been chosen for the task. I know this happened in my life years ago, many times and I failed to see God in the faces of those He sent to help me. I would regret that, except that Jesus has taught me not to linger over past regrets, because He isn't keeping a list of all of my failures. He's only celebrating my successes. He's only focused on loving me and lighting my path back to Him.

18

DAYS OF FUTURE PASSED

*A*s I grew older, I began to question a lot of things I was taught as a child, by my parents, but also in church. A lot of those things started to make less sense or seem less valid, once I began to rebuild my life after losing Ethan.

For many years, I just didn't question things much. I thought I had the answers to most of life's questions and those things I still questioned, I believed would be revealed after I left this life. I never thought very seriously about a pre-life. Why is it that so many of us believe strongly in an afterlife, but are not really able to consider the concept of a pre-existence?

Well, I guess, in my case I can start by saying, it wasn't what I was taught to believe in my home or in church. The teachings of our youth are extremely difficult for most of us to reject. It seems disrespectful in many ways to discard the beliefs our parents held so strongly and it seems nearly sacrilegious to question what was taught in our church.

Many people believe because reincarnation isn't specifically mentioned in the Bible, that it isn't a possibility. Jesus said in John 16:12, *"I have yet many things to say to you, but you cannot bear to hear them now. But, when He, the Spirit of Truth, is come, He will guide you into all truth."*

I believe reincarnation could be one of these unknown things the Holy Spirit will guide us to believe; but no one knows if that is so. I do believe the scripture makes it clear there are many things we don't yet know, so why would it make sense to pronounce judgement on this subject, without having all of the information necessary to make an informed decision?

Because this book deals a lot with examining memories; it raises the question in my mind as to whether all of our memories are associated with current lives or if they could be something retained from a previous incarnation? There are documented cases of people who seem to be remembering former lives in amazing and often verifiable detail. Much research has been done on this subject, and while it's possible to fool even the experts, it isn't an easy thing to do. For instance, many of these stories include names, dates, places, spouses, children etc. All of those things can be easily checked out and either verified or disproven.

I'm not saying the Bible is false in anyway; just that we may not have all of the information on a variety of subjects. My only objection to belief in reincarnation, is the teaching of my youth. I do believe, it could answer a lot of difficult questions, that no other satisfactory answer can be found for.

I have endeavored, since the first moments of my spiritual search for truth, to not allow myself to be led down a rabbit hole, by some false teacher or false belief. I pay very close attention to my recurring thoughts and after I become convinced of their validity and that acting on them would not cause harm to myself or anyone else; I often act on them. The idea of reincarnation has become a recurring theme; in spite of my having tried to logically dismiss it. It remains for me, a possible explanation for many things and if and when my spirit comes to a place of acceptance and peace with it; I will know the idea is valid.

Let me present to you some of the things I think reincarnation might be an explanation for:

I'm sure you have questioned, as I have, why anyone is born with a physical handicap? Why are children born blind, or with a heart condition, or without a brain? It's nearly impossible to believe that a loving God would allow such a thing to happen. Many people who believe in God, struggle with questions such as this.

There is only one constant and unchangeable thing that exists anywhere; that is God. I know God is love; that has been proven to me repeatedly over the course of the past 5 years. I also know that as Love, He can't produce pain or evil or darkness. I believe those things exist in some form, but they are man-made. So, the answer can't be that He doesn't care about these children, in whom He has implanted a spark of His own Spirit. I also don't believe these things happen as retribution for some failing in the parents; a loving God would not and could not punish one spirit by hurting another. The Bible says that each of us is precious in the sight of God and that it isn't His will that any should come to harm. It also says the very hairs of our heads are numbered and that God has a plan to prosper us and not to harm us.

In light of all of this, wouldn't the fact that each spirit could be incarnated numerous times in order to experience life from different perspectives, be a reasonable and acceptable answer. It's a lot to think about.

19

WHISPERING HOPE

*I*n early December of 2001, my mother was dying of cancer; she was in the last few weeks of her earthly life. My sister and I devoted all of our time to caring for her at our parent's home. My son Ethan, was attending college in a place about an hour away from home. He and his wife Liz came home to visit us and to see his grandmother one last time. The next day, he wanted us to go see the first "Lord of the Rings" movie, that had just been released. I was really not in the mood for a movie and since we had to leave town to see it, I was very reluctant. Ethan really wanted to see it with us, so I agreed to go. I wasn't sure my nerves were up to it or that I had enough wits about me to focus on the story.

Ethan was still in elementary school when he discovered J.R.R. Tolkien's book, "Lord of the Rings". He instantly fell in love with it. It is actually a series of books that are often sold as a set. We bought him a nicely bound set for Christmas and he read it numerous times. I, myself, knew very little about the story until I sat down to watch the movies.

Life had gotten very serious with my mother's illness and fiction seemed trivial and pointless in those weeks before her passing. Since the moment we stood in her hospital room and a doctor quite matter-of-factly told her the cancer had spread and it was terminal, I had ceased to believe there was hope. That diagnosis meant there was no hope for my mother to recover and it was hard to believe hope could really be recovered for my family. My state of mind when I sat down in that theater, next to Ethan to watch the movie he was so excited about, was hopelessness.

In spite of myself, I began to be pulled into the story. It was total escapism and was probably exactly what I needed at the time; if only for a short period.

When the character Frodo, is wounded and near death, the only "hope" for saving him is to get him to the elves in time. Though the journey is impeded by some evil creatures, Frodo arrives in time and the magic of the elves saves his life. He is on a perilous journey to take the "one ring" back to the mountain where it was made and throw it into the fire to be destroyed. The ring was an evil thing that corrupted the hearts of even the strongest beings. It was a tool, used by an evil being to gain power and control over all of the peoples of "Middle Earth". Many times, over the course of telling this story, the heroic characters are in extreme danger and the audience, who has grown to love them and hope they are successful in their quest to save their world, fear they will be lost.

I began to see that Tolkien's story had a far deeper meaning. While it appears to be about wizards, elves, hobbits and rings, it is actually symbolic of life, with all its cruelty, greed, oppression and lust for power. As bad as that all seems, it is also about heroism, devotion, comradery, single-mindedness, sacrifice for the good of all, perseverance and even though it appears to be lost; it is in the end, a story about hope.

There is a scene in another of the movies in The Lord of the Rings" Trilogy, where a battle is about to be fought. The heroes are incredibly outnumbered and even old men and children are called in to fight for the survival of their people. The character "Aragorn", sits on a step mentally preparing to face what could be his final battle. The morale of all those around him has fallen to the deepest depths and fear is gnawing at all who have been called to fight. A young boy stands near him holding a sword that looks bigger than the child, himself. Aragorn calls to the boy to come closer to him and takes the sword from the child and examines it. The boy says, *"The men say the cause is lost; they say there is no hope."* Though in his heart Aragorn knows what the men have said may well be true; he heroically sets aside his own doubts and tells the child, who's eyes shine brightly with fear: *"there is always hope!"* Those words are probably my favorite bit of dialog in the whole series of movies. They come to me often in life; even when it appears foolish to continue to hope.

In the dark hours and days following the tragedy that took Ethan's life, God was my only hope of surviving the loss of my child. When life presents hopeless odds, or the certainty of loss and death rise up before us, God is there and in Him we can place our fear, our doubt, our sorrow and our devotion.

20

THOSE WERE THE DAYS

*I*n this time of increased uncertainty about nearly everything, the past seems a much more pleasant and safer place to rest our minds and hearts. There is little about the past that is unknown to us, the present is chaotic, at best, and the future is sometimes a fearsome prospect.

While we can't really "live" in the past, it is a wonderful place to visit and rest your mind and spirit; like a mental and spiritual vacation, if you will. The past is sort of like an old-fashioned jukebox. The kind where you could see the records spinning before the selection was made. You can "select" any memory you choose, at any given time. Memories come like singles (45's) or they can come like long playing albums (33-1/2). I realize I'll be leaving younger people behind, using this analogy, but even my children know about singles, albums and jukeboxes.

Some memories are just snippets of things, like a snapshot; a smile, a sleeping child, or a birthday cake with candles glowing. Other memories are like watching a video; you can mentally move through a remembered sequence of something as though it had been physically recorded. Memories don't require cameras or recording equipment to preserve them; they live in your mind and your heart.

When I was younger, I worked in a couple of different nursing home facilities and took care of numerous patients with Alzheimer's or another form of dementia. I remember one man, in particular; he had been a very skilled and successful dentist for many years. He had often served as an officer of many of the civic organizations he belonged to and was a past officer in the "Ducks Unlimited" organization, which is a group that conserves and creates natural habitats for water fowl. I know this because his family decorated his room at the nursing home with many awards and certificates he received for his service to that organization. In short, he was a very involved, vital and successful person in many avenues of life, before his illness progressed to a point that he couldn't remember any of these things. He couldn't even remember his own wife; he thought she seemed familiar, but believed she was his sister.

Doctors would probably say his memories were lost; I don't believe that. I believe they live in your heart as well as your mind; I believe they are still there even if you are unable to recall them.

I also believe that our memories are such a vital part of who we are, that they go with us into the next life. In the case of someone with Alzheimer's I believe they are fully restored in the heavenly realm.

Memories are our own personal history and just as with any other kind of history, they serve to remind us of previous mistakes and help us to avoid repeating them. They hold the history of every encounter we have ever had with another human being (spirit) and they allow us to relive the special and most precious moments of our lives.

If we choose, we can recall times of loss and pain, though

most of us avoid reliving those moments in time; they are often moments of significant growth and revelation.

We all have highs and lows in life and our memories reflect them. When my mother began to look back at her life, a few weeks before she passed, she determined, that on balance her life had been a good experience. When observing life "on balance", the highs and lows are both modified; the highs aren't as high and the lows aren't as low. It is this balance that creates the satisfaction we feel with having lived a "good", though not perfect life. In our final hours, money or position nor celebrity matter to us at all; their desirability was an illusion the world created for us.

"Be not conformed to this world; but be ye transformed by the renewing of your mind, that ye may prove what is the good, and acceptable, and perfect, will of God."

Romans 12:2

21

DREAM ON

*A*s I was editing the chapter," Those Were the Days", the thought came to me that there are multiple kinds of dreams and each must have a specific purpose. There are times that memories show up in our dreams; often they are mingled with what appears to be fiction created by our brain, during deep sleep. Sometimes, dreams are woven around some real problem you are experiencing and you are problem solving in your sleep. Sometimes, we receive Divine messages in our dreams. There is a science that is devoted to the study of dreams; it is called Oneirology. This research only studies the process of dreaming and does not involve dream interpretation. Many of us are fascinated by dreams; I fall into that group. Perhaps, you may think that dreams are just a way our brain entertains itself while we are sleeping and it is bored? Many people believe the brain is actively organizing our thoughts as we sleep, and there is no meaning in this at all. I think dreams can probably be all of these things at various times.

We know from reading the Bible that God frequently used dreams to convey messages or give direction to certain people. The most easily recalled recipient of these dreams is Joseph, the earthly father of Jesus. He was visited by the angel Gabriel several times; each time he was given an important directive. In the first dream, Joseph learned that Mary was indeed carrying the unborn Messiah, as she claimed. In the second, he was told to hastily rise in the night and take Mary and Jesus to Egypt, to protect The Holy Child from Herod. In the third dream, he was informed that Herod had died and it was safe to return home and that they should go to Nazareth, which was a fulfilment of the prophecy.

Just as I have learned to pay close attention to my recurring thoughts, I also pay attention to recurring dreams; some of them started when I was very young. Some of them began to occur after the passing of a loved one; I never dreamed about my mother until she passed away. In my recurring dream, she is alive, though changed; she is younger and seems to be more spirit than human being. She is always across the room from me and there is a physical barrier between us. Only once has she spoken and that was through telepathic communication. She said: *"I am not really far away from you."*

Most of my recurring dreams are pleasant, but there are a few exceptions. As a child, I began to have a dream about driving a car over an open bridge. I knew I was too small to drive the car and couldn't see over the steering wheel. Nonetheless, I knew I was supposed to do it. The bridge was really just a couple of wooden planks with no sides and nothing connecting them to each other. There was water under the bridge and I sensed it was very deep. I could never see the end of the bridge or a bank on the other side. The dream was always very brief, because almost immediately the car began to plunge into the water below and I would wake up.

I can't remember exactly when I first had this dream, but it's possible that it began after my father's oldest sister drowned in a boating accident. I would have been around 5 yrs. old. When I was 6 or 7, my mother enrolled me in swimming lessons. I was terrified and never really learned to swim well. I still have a fear of bodies of water. I don't think I've had this dream since I learned to drive.

I really am convinced dreams are meaningful in some way, because I believe everything in life has meaning; I am curious enough to want to find the meaning in all things.

22

WHERE NO ONE STANDS ALONE

None of us is privileged to know how long our time here will be. I'm referring to our natural life span, the one that is part of God's plan for our spirit's life as a human being. Our society leads us to assume we will all live to be well-advanced in years, before the call comes for us to depart. We also sometimes, assume that those born into this world first, will be the first to leave it; following the birth order. I guess in some sense that's logical, but rarely does it happen that way.

Parents usually assume they will leave before their children and that the elder of the two will go first; sooner than the spouse. Children usually assume their parents will predecease them and that the eldest sibling will go first.

In my own family situation, almost none of these things has gone as assumed. For instance, my father was 4 yrs. older than my mother; cancer took her at the age of 72, while my father lived past his 90th birthday. He was shocked because he expected to go first for a couple of reasons: He was older, his own father passed at 68 and if you look around you see many more widows than widowers.

My husband and I did not expect to outlive any of our children; our son who passed was the youngest, not the oldest of the three.

My husband's brother who recently passed, was 15 yrs. younger and was the 4th of 5 siblings born to his parents; my husband is the oldest sibling.

Just these few examples show us that it's probably not safe to assume anything on the subject of longevity.

My friend, Raven passed, unexpectedly at the age of 29; her heart simply stopped for no apparent reason. I was stunned by her loss and horrified to think that someone who had just had a yearly physical and deemed to be healthy, could just go to sleep and be whisked away, for no apparent reason.

I began to have panic attacks and I grew increasingly afraid to go to sleep. Exhaustion from lack of sleep threw my emotions into a state of complete turmoil. Anyone who has never had a panic attack probably doesn't understand the terror they cause, even when there's nothing obvious to be afraid of.

I began to think about dying all of the time and it effected my actions every moment. For instance; I wouldn't even leave home to go to the grocery store 4 blocks away from my house, without making sure everything was in place, in the event something happened to me and I never returned.

I was put on medication that slowed my heart rate and everything began to look like it was foggy; I felt like I was moving in slow motion. I decided that wasn't a satisfactory solution to the problem and I stopped taking it. I was afraid it would just stop my heart altogether.

I gave up anything that had caffeine in it, because it is a known trigger for panic attacks. After months of living with this unreasonable fear, I asked God to remove it from my life and they gradually left me.

I learned through this experience, that you can't live your

life focused on dying. That doesn't mean you can totally dismiss the fact that we all face the end of our human existence at some point; it just means if you dwell on death you can't focus on life and that is the point of us being here; to live.

When my mother was diagnosed with cancer, long before we were told it was terminal. She made the statement that she didn't think she would live much longer; I think she could sense it. I tried to encourage her to think positively and I said to her, *"We don't know that; we're just going to live until there's no more living to be done!"*

When my son's life was taken, I wasn't sure I could go on living and initially, I wasn't sure I wanted to; the pain was excruciating. For many months, I would force myself to get out of bed in the morning and I would ask God this question, *"How long will I have to live without my son?"* I never got a direct answer to that question, but God was working through my newfound relationship with Jesus and the Holy Spirit and one day I realized I was asking a different question, *"How long will You let me live, to tell the world what you have done for me?"* Somehow, my overwhelming grief had transformed into gratitude. It will always hurt that Ethan is not living his life here with us, but I know he is living and that fact isn't even debatable in my mind and heart.

I began to realize there is a purpose for every life, even if it isn't obvious what it might be and that each life must be lived to the end of it's allotted time on Earth. Ethan lived a lot more in his forty years than many people do in twice that time. That is a blessing! I will see my son again, when my own life here is complete. In the meantime, I am meant to make my life as meaningful as I can.

My hope is that I won't have to see the ones I love, go before me. That isn't likely, but if it should happen that way, I know

God would give me courage and strength. Even through the weight of unbearable grief, we never stand alone.

" I will not leave you comfortless; I will come to you."

John 14:18

"Let not your heart be troubled, neither let it be afraid."

John 14:27

23

HE STOPPED LOVING HER TODAY

*T*raditional Christian wedding vows read: "Till death do us part"; at that point the responsibilities of marriage end. Jesus said in Matthew 22:30: *"At the resurrection people will neither marry; nor are given in marriage, but are as the angels of God in heaven"*. Apparently, there is no need for marriage in heaven, but does this mean the love of husbands and wives dies when the physical body ceases to function? No, I don't believe it does.

When the first blush of romance subsides a bit and gives way to the serious business of truly becoming one, love deepens and undergoes a process that could be compared to alchemy; such as when lead is turned into gold. This magic doesn't occur in all marriages, but I believe it's supposed to. When it does, it's a beautiful thing to behold, and neither time nor death can tarnish or destroy it. It can take years for this miraculous process to be completed, but then maybe it's never finished.

This kind of marriage goes through the same trials and heartaches any other marriage endures, but it isn't weakened by these things; it is purified instead. Every loss or disaster only strengthens and polishes the bond these two people share. Though they may sometimes falter or stagger under the weight of life's burdens, they cling to each other, supporting each other in their times of weakness and walk hand in hand out of the darkness and into the light. They are stronger together, but even when apart their love for each other strengthens and encourages them.

People often joke that old married couples start to look alike. If that's so, it's probably because they are kindred spirits. Many couples begin to finish each other's sentences and often, don't even need to converse out loud to know how the other is feeling or what the other person is thinking. They can just read each other with near faultless accuracy. The old saying: *"Familiarity breeds contempt,"* has no application here.

My own parents didn't always agree verbally, in fact, they bickered a lot, which they were pretty unaware of. They were musicians and they shared the language of music in a way they each understood, without the need for words. That connection carried them through many disappointments, losses and tragedies. They shared 54 years of marriage, before my mother passed away. My father was lost without her and we were surprised when he remarried, but he had been miserable alone. He survived my mother by 13 years, and there is no doubt in my mind, that he went to heaven still very much in love with her and I'm just as sure she was waiting there to greet him.

I have previously quoted our former minister, Jim, and once more something he used to say comes to mind, it is this: *"The way to have a strong, committed marriage is to keep your eyes on each other and no place else."* If your greatest concern is for the health, happiness and well-being of the one you married, and theirs is the same for you, there is truly nothing on this earth that can separate you or destroy the love you have for each other. Such a love is a gift from God and it is also a gift to Him.

24

WHAT'S YOUR MAMA'S NAME?

*B*y the time my mother was 5 years old, her immediate family unit had disintegrated. She was born in August of 1929; it was the eve of the Great Depression. She and her brother were sent to live with their aunt and uncle, who became their legal guardians. Her parents divorced and her mother remarried and left the state. Her father left the area to try to find work. He tried to see his children whenever he was back in town to visit his parents and siblings, but he wasn't allowed to see my mother or her brother. The aunt and uncle were a childless couple who wanted to raise the children as their own and were afraid their father would try to take them away. My mother didn't see her father again until she was about 32 years old.

One day when I was about 7 or 8 years old; I came home from school and found my mother sitting in our living room, talking to a man I had never seen before. She introduced him to me as her father, my grandpa.

Aunt Anna lived just half a block down the street from us and she often popped in during the day. She never knocked, because she was family; she would just open the door and come in. She did just that while our visitor was still there. She took one look at him, turned on her heel and slammed the door after her as hard as she could.

I was completely astonished at the whole scene. We had been told almost nothing about my mother's family and early life; we did know that she grew up at Anna and Richie's house and that her mother lived in Texas. I don't remember even thinking to ask where her father was. It was always clear that she didn't like to talk about her family.

I don't remember my grandfather coming to the house again after that; he knew it would cause problems for our mother. He lived at a local hotel for a couple of years. Sometimes in the evening we would go for a ride in the car. If he was sitting outside, my Dad would stop and Mother would talk to him from the window.

I was old enough that my mother would sometimes send me to town to pick up things she needed. My mother never learned to drive, so unless Dad was home from work it was hard for her to get what she needed during the day. The hotel where Grandpa Howard lived was in the downtown area and often, he would be sitting outside. If he saw me on either side of the street, he would call or motion for me to come over to where he was. He always wanted to give me a nickel for an ice cream cone. My mother told me not to take his money, because he had so little to live on. If I refused to accept the nickel, he would look so sad that I wanted to cry. When I explained that to my mother, she said it was ok every now and then, but not to do it too often. He only wanted to buy a treat for his little granddaughter, who knew so little of him; it made him happy and I don't think he had much in his life to be happy about.

After a couple of years, he got really sick and mother told us he had stomach cancer and he was dying. When he was in the county hospital my dad would drive us there on Sunday afternoons and Mother would go in alone and visit him. During this time, my mother was pregnant with my youngest sister. It had been a difficult pregnancy and she wasn't feeling very well. She would come out of the hospital and often vomit before she got in the car, because it upset her so much to see him in the condition he was in. He died a few months later.

Years after he passed, my grandmother told me he had been a good man and a kind husband to her. He was a number of years older than she was and she had married him because he had a job and she thought he could take care of her. Then the Depression hit and there was no work to be had. She and Howard could no longer provide a home for their children, so they took them to her sister Anna's house, because her husband Richie, had several ways of making money and they knew they would be cared for. Grandma said, she wanted a better life and she became involved with her second husband. She regretted never being able to take her children to live with her.

I've always felt bad that my mother only got to spend such a short time getting to know her father and then he was gone again. She appreciated all that Anna and Richie had done for her and her brother, but it was a difficult relationship to the end. As with most children of divorce, she felt loyal to everyone and that tore at her heart.

When Grandpa Howard came home to reconnect with his family, he was a worn-down old man; probably not as old as his appearance suggested. We have only one tiny picture of him that was taken in a photo booth. We never saw him as a young man and much of his life story is a blank page. I remember him as a sad, but kindly old man.

I believe every person has a story; not all stories are pleasant;

but they each have meaning and I find it sad when a spirit passes from this world and so much of their story is left untold. The important thing about ancestors is this: if any one of them in your direct lineage had made a different decision about where to live, who to marry, or not to have children, many of us wouldn't exist as the people we are.

As my life review progresses, my mind becomes more fixed on the people from my past. I try to see them as the spirit that lived inside the human beings they were. Some of them, I never knew and some of them I knew so early in my life that I lacked the emotional and spiritual maturity to see them other than as they appeared to my worldly senses.

I often wonder if it's possible for us to discover our spiritual senses earlier than most people do or if that can only come with a certain level of maturity. Perhaps, the wisdom that comes with age, can't be found any other way.

25

SWEET DREAMS

My Mother and Father married when she was 18 yrs. old. In spite of her young age, she was already pursuing her dream of singing professionally. She appeared many times in local variety shows and talent contests. She also had a radio show at a small station in a nearby town, where she worked as a disc jockey, playing all of the latest country western recordings.

She met my father because she needed a guitar player who could play melody while she played rhythm. Someone at the restaurant where she worked, told her they knew a guy who was working right across the street who could help her out. They married about a year later and she still intended to pursue her dream of being a singer. By 1955, they had three young children and her dream began to take a back seat to motherhood and caring for a home; still the dream never died. They made friends with other local musicians and for a number of years, nearly every weekend saw us playing outside at someone else's house until late in the evening, as the adults made music and the kids played tag and red rover.

When my father began to recognize a calling to be a lay minister, serving at various little country churches, her dream began to clash with the traditional role of a minister's wife. She felt a bit betrayed because she hadn't signed on to be the minister's wife, but in the end, she supported his calling and often provided special music during the services where he preached.

She looked for appropriate places to sing and sometimes entertained at lodge meetings or for ladies' groups. Once she coerced my brother and me to sing with her at a lodge meeting. She had to promise me a new dress; singing publicly did not come as naturally to me as it did for my Mother. She had much more confidence on a stage performing, than at any other time or in any other place.

In the last few years of her life, she convinced my Father to turn a large shop area on their property, into a music theater, so she had a place to perform. They had local guest musicians and a small, but faithful audience who enjoyed the weekend performances. She was in her element, even though it took most of their time the following week to prepare for the next show. She enjoyed the theater for a couple of years and then cancer began to take her strength and her health began to fail. She could no longer put so much energy into the theater, but she never lost her love of singing.

One day, a few weeks before her passing, we had some of the grandkids visiting at Mom's and over the course of the afternoon, people began to gravitate out to the theater. By this time, Mother was basically unable to be out of bed. She asked me to put her in the wheelchair and take her out to the theater; it was a struggle, but I got her out there.

On the stage was a set of drums that belonged to my brother's best friend, Steve, who sometimes sat in on performances. My sister's husband, Audie, is a drummer and Mother asked him to play a solo for her. He played a solo that rattled all of the windows in the building and she loved it. When I got her back to her bed, she was exhausted, but happy; her dream never died, but life altered it a lot. In the end, she knew she had been given a lot of other wonderful things in her life to compensate for the dream that was never totally realized.

Nearly all of us have a dream or vision of what we want our life to be; rarely does life follow the exact path we imagine. It doesn't necessarily follow that life is a disappointment because of that. Many times, the reality of our lives is better than it would have been had our entire vision been realized. It may take some time and perspective, before we realize that fact, but people often do come to that realization before they reach the end of life here.

My dream was to become a mother; I was given three sons and they are my crowning achievement. It wasn't part of my dream to lose one of them, during my lifetime, but it happened, nonetheless. At first, I thought my dream had been destroyed, when Ethan's life was taken. That could have become my reality, but I couldn't go on living if I had let his loss ruin everything my husband and I had worked so hard to build; Ethan would hate that. I asked God to help me find a way to live in spite of such a devastating loss. Instead of becoming bitter, God helped me to become grateful for all I had been given. The fact that it had been taken away, didn't change the fact that I received the gift of Ethan's life, through my own. Yes, it still hurts that he's not here with us physically, but I wouldn't have missed a moment of having him in my life for nearly forty years. God has allowed me to feel Ethan's spirit with me every day and to hear his voice in my own spirit.

It's good to have dreams and goals for your life, but you need to allow for the changes life will interject along the way. If you will allow it, God will give you the best gifts you could ever receive. He wants you to be happy, but sometimes the road to happiness isn't the first one you choose.

My mother, Marie, performing in a talent show.

26

HEAVENLY SUNSHINE

*W*e are all children of the same God: created in His image, yet we are not identical. We are different is appearance, temperament, intellect and spirit. We do not all grow spiritually at thc same pace or in the same way. We do not all have the same aptitudes, but I believe, spiritually, we are all teachable, in the end. It may take some of us a lot longer to arrive in the optimal place a spirit should or could be. Because we have free-will, our choices can determine what path in life we take. Some of us walk our own path all of our lives, never suspecting that it leads us nowhere. Some of us recognize Divine guidance, but stubbornly refuse to alter our course. Some of us give lip service to the guidance we receive, but inwardly, resist relinquishing our need to control our own destiny. Only in surrendering our resistance to God's perfect will for our lives, do we open the door to the amazing plans He has for us.

So many of us make life much harder than it is meant to be, because we try to swim upstream. We wear ourselves out, resisting the natural course. If we stop resisting, the path can be revealed to us through heavenly communication. This communication can come in many forms: dreams, recurring thoughts, ideas that pop into our minds from nowhere, or through the "still small voice" we only are able to hear when we are peaceful, calm and still.

As a child, I always wanted to make flowers grow. I planted seeds a number of times; sometimes nothing sprouted. Occasionally, tiny green seedlings would push up through the soil and I would be delighted, but then I would forget to water them and the plants would wither and die. Sometimes, I would water them too much and they would turn yellow and die. Over the years, I've learned to give them what they need to thrive, but even with a lot more knowledge than I had as a child, my efforts are not always successful. Sometimes, even if I have done everything just right, the plants are attacked by insects or fungus and they die. When that happens, I try to correct the problem, so they can begin to thrive.

Our spirits are just like plants; some of us need more of one thing than another in order to thrive. Some of us will flourish easily and some will struggle. I think, God sometimes, allows us to decide where we will put down our roots and He expects us to learn how to make the necessary changes that will help us grow into a beautiful specimen. He never leaves us entirely on our own and often whispers advice in our ear; our task is to learn to hear His voice and to listen and respond.

In Matthew 13:1-9, Jesus tells a story that is known as the Parable of the Sower of Seeds. A parable is a simple story designed to teach a moral lesson. In the story a man is sowing seeds; some fall on the path that is hardened from people walking there. It sat on top of the soil and the birds ate it. Some seeds fell on rocky soil, they sprouted, but the sun burned up the tender seedlings. Some seeds fell into thorny bushes, that soon grew up and choked the plants. Some seed fell on good soil and the plants thrived and produced grain.

This story is about life and our human response to God. The seeds are opportunities for spiritual growth. God offers them to us all, but some are ignored (like those the birds ate). Some wither (like the seeds that fell on rocky soil). Some sprout and begin to grow, but the thorns of life (temptations that pull our focus back into the world) choke them out.

I believe our time on Earth is designed to help us grow spiritually; we are, after all, spirits having a human experience. I believe the ultimate plan for each spirit, is to reach the highest level of illumination and that it can take many lifetimes for that to be accomplished. It makes no sense to me that we are all imbued with a spirit at birth and some spirits live such a short human life. It's hard to see that as an opportunity for total illumination. It's also hard to see God ever rejecting any spirit that is His own creation and is inherently a part of His being. I think God (the sower of seeds) plants those spirits over and over again, until they reach the optimum level of growth and there are no more lessons to be taught. He is the Sunshine and the Rain that helps them grow.

27

WHERE HAVE ALL THE FLOWERS GONE?

*W*e are living through a time of great human tragedy; the Covid 19 pandemic. The loss of life is staggering; at least it should be, but for many it isn't; that is a great tragedy in itself. Someone recently noted, when the death toll in this country alone, reached 178,000, it would be like walking into the city of Topeka and finding it a ghost town; not one single survivor. The death toll at this point has far exceeded that horrific number and it shows no signs of slowing. Here are a few other examples of familiar cities with similar population to Topeka: Rochester N.Y., Akron, Ohio, Little Rock Ar., Amarillo, Tx., Pasadena, Ca. Imagine any one of these places being completely depopulated. It should be a sobering thought for all of us, but it doesn't seem to be for many; I find that deeply disturbing.

Each of the deaths from Covid- 19, represents a human being, a real person, with loved ones, and friends; people who love them and need their presence here. The enormity of these losses is unfathomable and yet many only see a number that has little impact on them personally. Where is our humanity? Are we so desensitized that we are unable to respond?

You may be one who says: *"Well, it doesn't do any good to dwell on these things!"* To that, I would say that there's a lot of space between dwelling on a tragedy and giving it the proper respect before moving on.

When you see the disregard and disrespect of life by so many, it is disheartening. I believe these tremendous losses will impact us whether we choose to recognize it or not. We are all interconnected, because we dwell on this planet together for a period of time and we will all return to the place of our origin, at some point. A loss such as this can't help but have some impact on the universe we live in and a price will be paid whether we choose to acknowledge its connection to this pandemic or not. My hope is, that when I leave here, I will have left the world better, because I walked on it for a time. Most of us will never do anything to cause a cosmic shift, but every act of love or kindness or thoughtfulness flows together to help maintain a spiritual balance. That balance depends on small and seemingly unimportant acts, by the little known or celebrated among us. If you feel there is little you can do, you are mistaken.

"Truly I tell you, whatever you did for one of the least of these brothers and sisters of mine, you did for Me."

Matthew 25:40

28

SAD EYES

*W*e all experience change in our lives; usually change occurs so gradually it is nearly imperceptible, as it's happening. You just wake up one day and realize that you're different; you look different or feel different. Perhaps, your thoughts, ideas, or opinions have changed. We accept these gradual changes as a naturally occurring thing.
Sudden changes can be much harder to process. As I review my own life, I can see several instances of very sudden and surprising change.

The first sudden change that comes to mind, precipitated the end of my first marriage. I have spoken briefly in other books about my very early marriage, at the age of 17, and the depression and deep sense of failure I experienced when it ended in divorce 5 yrs. later. Without going into too much detail, I will just say that the beginning of the end came like a bolt of lightning from out of a blue sky.

One night after I had been married a little over a year and thought my life was really good, my husband said something to me that rocked my world completely. I must explain that one of the reasons I wanted to get married so young, was that I felt unloved. I was looking for someone to love me completely and unconditionally; someone who would make me feel special. I felt the same way when I had my first child, before I was 18; I believed if I had children and I treated them lovingly, they would also love me unconditionally. I didn't understand at that time, how important it is to love yourself first and what a positive impact that has on every other relationship you create.

When my husband said those words that still live in my distant, mostly untouched memories of that marriage, I nearly stopped breathing. I felt like I'd been kicked in the chest. Those few sentences brought my illusion of happiness crashing to the ground; I was devastated. In seconds, the love I felt for him completely evaporated. It was like turning off a light switch; it was all gone. I asked him to repeat what he had said, just in case I was misunderstanding him. I asked him a couple of questions about it and that confirmed that I had understood him precisely. I didn't know what to do.

I struggled on in that marriage for a further 4yrs. but the damage was done and there was no way to fix it. No matter how hard I tried to live with my mistake, I knew it was over. During those 4 yrs. I was miserable and seriously depressed. I'd like to say here for those of you who don't know; misery is just as painful; even when you've created it yourself. I felt trapped in the wrong marriage. I had taken my marriage vows very seriously and when I stood before God and 200 witnesses and promised to be with my husband until I died; I meant every word. I had never made a promise to God before and I wasn't sure where I'd be if I broke it. Somehow, in all of my religious training, the part about the loving and forgiving God didn't rise to the top.

I was so hurt and sick at heart and I made many mistakes during that time in my life. When I look back at that period of time, it seems as if it was someone other than myself who made all of those wrong choices. I was so hung up on breaking that one vow, that I ended up breaking several others while trying to avoid breaking that one. It is always so easy to see what you should have done, after the fact.

My husband and I separated several times and it was usually me who asked him to come back. I felt guilty depriving my sons of a father. They rarely saw him, even when he lived with us, but nevertheless, it seemed wrong. I had never been truly alone and it terrified me. I had no education beyond high school and no training of any kind. I struggled to provide for myself and my children.

Finally, I reached a level of depression that still frightens me today, when I think of how close I came to ending my life. One night, as I lay in bed, I realized I was thinking about how to take my life. This was a completely calm and very irrational conversation I was having with myself. It included things like: who would know how to fix my hair and do my makeup right and what would I want to wear for a funeral service.

Then, quite suddenly, I heard a very clear voice in my head say: HEY STUPID!! Are you listening to this? You can't do that; you brought two little boys into this world who need you in their lives and you owe it to them to stay here and figure it out!!This isn't about you anymore! Well, that certainly got my attention and I changed my focus from my own misery to what was best for my children. I began to see for the first time, how little my husband contributed to their welfare. I thought about what they were likely to learn from watching the way he chose to live his life. I decided I didn't want that for them. As for my reservations about breaking my promise to God; I knew I had to, but I didn't think He would accept it or forgive it. I was pretty sure God was through with me, at that point.

Once again, my life totally changed in that moment. I knew

what I had to do and I had the courage and resolve to do it.
Getting out of the marriage and finding a way to take care
of my children didn't happen as quickly, but within about 9
months, I got a divorce, moved into my parent's home and
found a job in the same town I lived in; even though jobs were
very scarce there.

Then some really amazing things began to happen in my life.
Looking back, I can see God's hand in finding that job and it
was there that I met my husband of 46yrs. who is without a
doubt, a gift from God. We met 3 days before I went to court
for my divorce hearing and were married 10 months later.
Eleven months after we married, Ethan was born; a child I
never believed I would have. I have so much to be grateful for!'

29

BIRTHDAY

*A*nother major shift in life occurred when I had my 60th birthday. The family I grew up in didn't really celebrate birthdays. We always got a present from our parents and each of us had a birthday party; not a party each year, just one party; period.

My one family party occurred just before I started kindergarten. I didn't know any of the kids I was going to be in school with, so my mother decided to invite the whole kindergarten class to my party. It was a bit odd having a whole bunch of strangers come to celebrate my birthday. I was very shy and was pretty overwhelmed; I spent most of my time with the kids from our neighborhood that were also invited.

When I was 14, some of my friends had a birthday party for me. They baked a cake and each one gave me something of theirs' that was special to them. I still have a pretty sugar bowl, after all these years, that my friend Rosie gave me; it belonged to her grandmother and I couldn't believe she was willing to part with it, but she said she had lots of things that belonged to her Grandmother and she wanted me to have it.

This brings me to my 60th birthday party and the biggest birthday surprise I've ever received. The party itself was a surprise; Ethan planned it with help from my sister Jeanne and our best friend Debra. My birthday is August 29, right before Labor Day weekend. For years Tom and I had a family picnic for our extended family at the city park. The kids came home for it every year, so when everyone showed up at my house, I just thought they were there for the picnic. I was part owner of an antique shop at that time and I had to work that day. I was really beat at the end of the day and just wanted to go home and sit down. Then, Ethan called and said everyone wanted to go to a local restaurant and bar for supper; I protested, but he wouldn't take no for an answer. I remember feeling very inappropriately dressed when I walked in the door and realized it was a birthday party and there were lots of people there to celebrate with me, as the honored guest.

The party was fun and I got to see some very good friends I hadn't seen for a long time. I went home exhausted and fell into bed. I don't think I moved a muscle all night. I woke in the morning and almost instantly new a metamorphosis had occurred. I was suddenly not the person I had known myself to be for many years. It was a shock because I rarely ever changed my attitudes or opinions about anything, and rarely did that happen for no apparent reason. To this day the only way I can account for it is spiritually; I believe it was preparation to help me survive the sudden and devastating loss of my son. That loss didn't occur for another 4 yrs. after the birthday party, but as I look back on those intervening years, I can see a number of things that seem pertinent to the spiritual preparation I was unaware of at the time.

You might ask, as I have many times, why did this preparation happen to me and not to millions of others who have suffered a similar loss. The only clue I have about that is that I feel, to my core, that I have a spiritual assignment to complete before I leave here. Without Divine intervention at the time of Ethan's passing; I truly believe I wouldn't be here to complete whatever this mission is. I did not initiate any of the spiritual experiences that I have to call miracles, that have occurred as a steady stream of unexplained events, since the day after my 64th birthday party.

The most profound spiritual experience of my life, is without question the transfiguration I witnessed on the day of Ethan's celebration service. When I looked into the eyes of Jesus and He spoke to me telepathically, I was instantly and forever changed.

Months after Ethan's life was taken, I had another profound experience, when I visited the National Cathedral in Washington, D.C. During a communion service in a small chapel under the main sanctuary; I was given a purpose for my life; a mission that gave me a clear path to living a meaningful and productive life. Since that day, I have received Divine guidance regularly; I never have to wonder long what my next step will be, the path is laid out before me a step at a time.

I am given words of Truth and wisdom to speak boldly; not of myself and my own knowledge apart from this spiritual guidance. It is only through that which comes to me, that which is given to me, that I can speak with courage and strength, without doubt and misgiving.

"Apart from me you can do nothing"

John 15:5

30

HEAR THE VOICE OF MY BELOVED

*T*his chapter relates to an event I've previously written about; my encounter with Jesus on the day of my son's burial. I'd like to elaborate on the message I received from Jesus that day. The title of this chapter is a bit deceiving, because what I want to get across to you who read this is, that I heard no voice; there was no audible sound. I understand it's confusing to say I "heard" something and then to say there was no sound. Therein lies some of the difficulty in trying to put a spiritual experience into clearly understandable language. So here is what actually happened that day:

I "perceived" the message without any words being spoken. Jesus mouth did not move and I heard no audible voice. The message I received was in two parts. Part one was: *"I'm here; I've always been here."* The way I described the second part of the message in my book "Learn To Be Still", is that Jesus nodded toward Ethan's casket. When I wrote that chapter, I struggled as to how to best relate what actually happened. What is more accurate to say, is that without Him having moved His head or His eyes, I "perceived" that His focus had changed and He was now talking about Ethan. What I received from Him, without sound was; *"I have him; he's with me and he's just fine. So, don't you worry about him."* In LTBS I used the words "telepathic communication" to describe what I heard. That still doesn't seem to exactly describe the experience, but I'm afraid it's as close as I can come with human language.

When I hear Ethan speaking to me, it's very similar to the experience I had in the cemetery. I hear thoughts that I know are not my own and I perceive they are from Ethan. Even though I can add the sound of Ethan's voice, because it is so familiar to me, I am not actually hearing him speak.

The same thing happens when I communicate with the Holy Spirit: a thought that is not my own suddenly pops into my head. These are not my own thoughts because they seem to come from slightly behind me and I often do not agree with them. For example: when the Holy Spirit began to plant thoughts of my forgiving the person who took Ethan's life, I wasn't ready to even consider that. I told God I wouldn't say no to the idea, but that I didn't know if I would ever be able to do that. At the very least, I thought it would take many years for that to happen. Through the prompting of the Spirit, it happened about 6-7 months after Ethan's passing.

Often when I pray for an opportunity, such as a way to be able to share my story more broadly; something very similar will happen, an idea will suddenly come to me. I perceive words, but there is no audible sound.

Many times, when I'm writing, there is a sudden shift from my own thoughts, to words that are like listening to dictation; here also, there is no sound. The words often come so quickly I am scribbling to keep up with what I'm hearing. When the speed suddenly increases and I don't recognize the words as my own, I'm instantly aware of the presence of another spirit.

The more detailed descriptions of events which I have previously related, that I am including in this book, are not a result of my wish to embellish my story; they are a result of the passage of time which has filled in a lot of missing pieces of information, that I was unable to recall initially. The initial shock wave that pulsed through my entire body when I received the news that my son had been murdered, was like a lightning strike; an intense bolt of energy shot through me and it was as if every nerve in my body fired at the same time. The lasting impact of that was loss of a huge portion of my memories and loss of ability to focus and retain new information without concerted effort on my part. In essence, I lived with what felt like brain damage for at least two years, following Ethan's passing. Over time, most of my lost memories have come back to me, but there are times that I still don't trust some of them. Often, if I question what I remember, I try to verify it through other people who share the same experience. As my memories and focus have come back, it often seems as if my life was a series of many black and white sketches and with time they are being filled in with color and detail.

For those of you who may be thinking that this accounts for the strange experiences I've had the past five years, I want to adamantly refute that idea. All of the spiritual experiences I have had were documented within minutes to hours of the time they occurred. I did this because, I knew I didn't want to rely on my seemingly damaged brain to recall them correctly. Many of my experiences are verifiable in other ways as well.

The transfiguration of my friend and Jesus left such an indelible mark that I am rarely able to think of it without being overcome with tears, gratitude and humility. My reaction to it after all this time, proves to me something incredible happened in those few moments that day in the cemetery.

My life has been transformed by these experiences that came to me from another place, that cannot be found or replicated by human beings or any knowledge that exists solely in this world. This is simply the truth, as honestly as I know how to present it.

31

THESE EYES

*O*nce again revisiting my encounter with Jesus; I would like to focus on aspects of His appearance. I guess I should say the aspects of my perception of His appearance. Judging by the many accounts I've read by others who've shared their personal encounters with Jesus, through an NDE (Near Death Experience) or other form of spiritual connection, I believe Jesus appears differently to each individual. I'm sure He can appear any way He chooses.

My experience with Jesus that day in the cemetery was very brief; though it seemed much longer than it likely could have been, this sense of timelessness, is a common component of NDE'S. As I have written in the chapter from my first book "Learn To Be Still", Jesus appeared to me through a transfiguration of another person whom I knew well. It occurred during the portion of my son's burial service that followed the final prayer; as those present filed past us to offer their condolences. There was only a brief pause in the flow of well-wishers, when someone stopped to talk to another family member who was sitting at the end of the front row. I was seated in the center of the front row. This pause caused a space of about 4 ft. between the person who had just passed by me and the person who temporarily stopped the line. The duration of this pause could only have been 15-20 seconds at the most. The telepathic communication that I shared with Jesus seemed much longer and the time His eyes were locked with mine, even longer than that.

His eyes are the most outstanding and unforgettable thing about Him. They are magnetic; charismatic. Revelations 2:18, reads: *"These things says the Son of God, who has eyes like a flame."* What I saw in Jesus eyes was light; it seemed like all of the energy of the Universe was contained in Him and by Him. That energy shone as light in His eyes.

The eyes of Jesus project toward you and at the same time they are pulling you into Him. They project a fierce compassion; I use the word fierce, not to describe a negative emotion, but to describe the depth of emotion. It was nearly overwhelming. They projected the same intensity of empathy, but the strongest emotion that is emitted from His entire presence is love. Philippians 2:10 reads: *"that at the name of Jesus every knee should bow, of those in heaven, and of those on earth, and of those under the earth."*

The presence of Jesus is so overwhelming and awe-inspiring, that your spirit is instantly humbled and the desire to fall at His feet overcomes you. He doesn't present a handsome countenance, but He is anything but ordinary; I don't recall ever seeing any other person who resembled Him in the slightest way. My point in describing Him physically, is that what is so overwhelming is His very presence, His "being", not His physical appearance.

32

HELP ME MAKE IT THROUGH THE NIGHT

Someday, I hope to be able to write a book that makes absolutely no mention of grief, but for now it's a subject that keeps coming up. There are various reasons to explain why I can't quite put this subject to rest. Perhaps, the biggest and most obvious reason is that my son was murdered; that's not something you just get over. That doesn't mean I can't talk about anything else, but I think it means I haven't fully explored this very important subject that impacts everyone at one time or another.

Another reason grief is still on my mind a lot, is the time we are living in right now; the time of the coronavirus pandemic. As I write this, over 4 million people in the world have died and for me the weight of those deaths hangs in the air; so much grief, so much loss. Because I have experienced a tragic loss myself, these losses are so much more to me than mere numbers.

Each of these people were living a life, they each had loved ones and friends who will never be the same without them. Most weren't able to be with their loved ones at the moment of their passing. Many have not received a proper burial. All of this weighs heavily on my heart. I cannot bear the burden of everyone else's grief; I know this, but it is still so hard not to be personally affected by it.

My husband recently lost his younger brother, Dan; grief once more hovers over us. Even though we are intimately acquainted with grief, it doesn't make it easier to have lost another loved one.

As I watch Dan's family deal with the reality of life without him, I am reminded of the minutes, hours and days of intense grief I experienced when Ethan was ripped out of our lives. I have examined grief from a myriad of angles, and my sad, but undeniable conclusion is: the only way to get through grief, is to go through grief. There are no easy outs, no shortcuts; grieving takes as long as it takes and it takes much longer than we ever imagine it will.

Grief is unpredictable; one day you feel sad, the next day empty, the next day nauseated and some people experience tremendous anger.

I know without doubt, that grief is an individual assignment; each person's experience is different and they must find their own way through it.
In spite of knowing that, I still feel compelled to share a few things that might help someone else who's struggling with grief. These are things that helped me make it through the hardest days.

The first and most important is a relationship with God; it doesn't have to be a perfect relationship; my own is testament to that. It doesn't have to be much of a relationship at all. In fact, as the song says (Just As I Am): it can be just as you are, with no excuses.

The second thing; also, extremely important, is what I would call a grief coach. If you think about it, we have coaches to help us get through many things in life. There are sports team coaches, Lamaze coaches, fitness coaches, etc. A grief coach is similar to each of these examples; it is someone who helps you to focus, is there to listen without judgement or criticism, to hold your hand, to cry with you, to reminisce with you and help you take each baby step toward healing.

A grief coach can be a professional counselor or a trusted friend or relative. I was fortunate to have my sister and friend, Jeanne, as my coach. She has several of the necessary qualities of a good counselor; she is a good listener and she's patient and calm.

The main point here is that you need to find someone you trust. Having another person to talk to helps you get your feelings out in the open; they can swim around in your head indefinitely. It can be a tremendous burden to keep them all inside; they are like built up steam in a pressure cooker, eventually the steam has to be released.

In addition to the many hours I spent sharing my thoughts and feelings with Jeanne, I began to keep numerous journals. I find writing to be very therapeutic for me; my early journals became my first book. Anything that will allow you to get your intense emotions out will be helpful.

I am still somewhat surprised that in spite of the oceans of tears I shed when Ethan's life was taken, I still get in a bit of a panic when I see those who are grieving, burst into tears. Even before my experience with deep grief, I was in a panic if someone burst into tears.

One afternoon during my mother's last few weeks of life, we were sitting in her living room; Jeanne and I and Dad were there and Mother was laying in the hospital bed, in the corner. I've mentioned in other places that they were both musicians and that they spent their entire 54 years of marriage making music together; it was what brought them together in the first place.

I thought it might help Mother to relax, if Dad played something for her on the autoharp; instead, she sat up and tried to sing along. She quickly realized she was far to weak and fell back onto the pillows. In that moment, they both understood that music was one more thing they were losing and they began to sob, simultaneously. I was horrified and I thought: *"Oh no, what have I done!"* I realized later, that they both needed to mourn their losses and crying was exactly what was called for at that moment.

I think it is very important that you not fight your feelings. The intensity of them serves a distinct purpose, even though it is hard to let go of what you instinctively feel you need to maintain control of. The turmoil in your heart and spirit will gradually subside and you will eventually regain some balance. It requires courage and patience to stand face to face with such strong emotions, but only when you've done it will you begin to live again.

"For you are my fortress, my refuge in times of trouble."

Psalm 46:1

33

STEPPIN' IN THE SLIDE ZONE

*F*ollowing Ethan's passing, I mourned not only his absence, but the loss of the life I had known with him present. I loved my life in the years prior to the tragedy that took him away; it was suddenly gone and I knew it could never be recaptured. If I was to go on living, it would have to be a different life to the one I had known. As a result of my efforts to recover and build a new life; I find myself now living in a "parallel" universe, so to speak. I'm not living physically on another planet or anything as strange as that sounds; I live every day in the world of "time", just like I always have, while simultaneously living or "walking" in the realm of spirit. I can't tell you exactly how I got to this place of parallel existence, I can only tell you some of the steps I took. Within a few weeks of losing Ethan, I began to read voraciously; it was almost a manic desire to find answers. In the beginning, it was fueled by my desire to discover anything and everything that was knowable about heaven; the place I knew Ethan's spirit had gone to. I read literally hundreds of books in a relatively short period of time. I read them all with a healthy dose of skepticism; I was searching for truth and my perception of truth had been dramatically empowered by what I had experienced. If I read something that just didn't ring true and I could find no peace with it, I discarded it.

The next thing I did, also rather obsessively, was to listen to music. I was hoping to hear Ethan speak to me again, as he did on the trip back from Mississippi, prior to his Celebration of Life service. At first, I thought I just had to wait for him to initiate the contact, but as time passed, I began to realize I could initiate communication with him myself. At first, this all happened through music; eventually I began to write letters to him and wait for a response. I have never written to him and not heard a response. As I have stated in earlier books, these communications are all telepathic. When I say I hear his voice; what that means is: I hear words in my head that are not my own thoughts; but there is no audible sound. I recognize the words as being Ethan's or sometimes the Holy Spirit's or sometimes they are the words of Jesus. I do not recognize a voice; I recognize an individual spirit. I know how crazy this sounds to other people, but I am attempting to be as truthful about my experiences as I can possibly be.

Stepping into this parallel place of existence is as easy now as it was to recognize when Ethan stopped speaking and the Holy Spirit stepped into our conversation. As I said, these two worlds exist simultaneously, they are parallel worlds of consciousness. I can be in one or the other or both at the same time; depending on where I put my focus. Stepping into the zone requires the use of senses other than those relied on in this world. They are spiritual senses and with practice they can become as finely tuned as human senses. Hearing messages from the "zone", utilizes a telepathic sense. Feeling spiritual presence utilizes a sense more difficult to accurately describe. The best I can do is to say it is acute awareness. These senses are easier to use when you are in a state of extreme relaxation and there is no resistance in your body.

In the world of time, we are generally aware of our surroundings; people, noises etc. this kind of awareness is stimulated by things outside your body, your human form. Spiritual awareness comes from within. Our inner awareness is impacted by our outward experiences and our databank of memories. These are only two of the resources that help to develop our spirituality. If we have had religious experiences without, they change us within and that also feeds our spiritual growth. Communicating with the Holy Spirit and receiving His guidance and teaching creates a very rich spiritual experience. Praying, meditating and listening for the voices of the three forms of the Trinity within yourself greatly accelerates your learning and becoming process. What are you becoming? You are becoming Christ-like within your spirit self.

When I am walking in the Kingdom, I don't leave the outer world entirely, but I become more of an observer of it than a participant in what is taking place there. I observe from a place of peace and I am working on making my observation as non-judgmental as possible. That is and always has been hard for me. Jesus said in John 14: 27-31
"Peace I leave with you; my peace I give unto you. Not as the world giveth, give I unto you. Let not your heart be troubled; neither let it be afraid. "The peace Jesus planted deep into my spirit is not easily disturbed. On the surface, I react to things that cause me fear or anxiety or anguish, much as I always did; but as I allow my consciousness to sink within myself, that peace awakens and begins to create light and warmth inside me, and I am able to say *"All will be well."*
Jesus meets me at this place of peace and I can walk into His embrace and know I am safe and I am loved. Since the day

of my son's burial when I looked into Jesus eyes; I am aware of His presence with me continually. Part of His message to me that day was: *"I am here; I have always been here."* Prior to that moment I had never felt His presence. When Jesus healed the blind beggar, he was given worldly vision; Jesus gave me spiritual vision that day at the cemetery.

When I began to look back at the life I lost when Ethan passed, I saw many times in my younger years, before Tom and I were married, when I had gotten myself into a mess by my own willful actions and then compounded those mistakes, by making even worse blunders. I thought God was really just observing us from afar and then judging how well we were handling our lives. I pictured Him up there somewhere, looking down with a disapproving frown creasing His brow and only when we had made such a tangled mess of things it was hopeless, He would step in, if we asked Him to.

There are a number of places in the Bible that tell us God is eager to help us if we will only ask Him and then get ourselves and our ego out of the way. God doesn't want to just observe our lives; He wants to experience life through us.

Many people learn how to utilize their spiritual senses as a result of a traumatic event, such as, a death or serious accident or illness. Others find their way to these untapped senses by determined effort to know the Truth.
In the way of trauma, a door opens to spiritual knowledge, as quickly as snapping your fingers. However, you must choose whether you will walk through the door and if you will use the tools you find waiting inside to search for the Truth and the answers you seek.

Finding access to the Truth through dedicated study and determination is a much slower process, but it leads to the same place and the same answers. I believe there are many paths and many portals; we do not all arrive on the same train, so to speak. Many religious teachings seem to want to quantify or limit access; I believe God is limitless and He doesn't reject anyone who seeks Him, no matter how long it takes or what road they traveled to get there. You are free to reject God at any time, if you choose to do that; He will never reject you. If you seek Him.

As you begin to step into the "zone" more and more frequently, things begin to happen regularly that confirm what Jesus told us about God and His kingdom.

As I began to communicate with Ethan after his passing, he said several times:" In the end, there is only Love." I have read or watched hundreds of accounts of NDE'S, and all were related by people who claim to know without any doubt, they visited the "kingdom" while being clinically de ceased. Much of what these people say mirrors my own experience and supports the things Ethan has related to me about where he is. Nearly everyone of these people say that the sense of unconditional Love is the most impressive thing about the place they visited.

"And now these three remain: faith, hope, and love, but the greatest of these is love."
1 Corinthians 13:13

34

ON THE TURNING AWAY

Tom and I were married in 1974 and in 1975, several months before Ethan was born; Tom legally adopted my two young sons, Brett and Jeff. So, when I talk about our sons, they truly are "our" sons. He committed to them, as well as to me, before we were even married. He made that commitment a solemn vow on the day the adoption papers were signed. We both agreed that we wanted our children to be raised in church and we began attending the local Christian Church when the kids were still pretty young.

We attended that church for about twenty years. I loved the people who attended there and enjoyed the services, but I began to feel as if I was just going through the motions, like a lot of people who fill pews every Sunday morning. I felt I needed something deeper, something that would touch me in a more spiritual way. I left the church; my husband continued to attend there for nearly another twenty years. At one point, the pastor dropped in for a visit and asked me if I had left the church because of him. I told him, in all honesty, that he was not the reason for my departure. I didn't attend church regularly again, until after Ethan's passing.

My intention when I left the church, was to pursue the

spiritual enrichment I felt was missing in my life, but exactly the opposite thing happened; I moved farther from God than I had at any time since my divorce. I still had a strong belief and I lived a pretty clean life, but I was not focused on or devoted to my faith for many years. I rarely prayed; I didn't expect to hear God's voice, and I didn't. When I think about my spiritual life during those years it just seems like a void. I was happy with my life, but I was still spiritually empty.

Then came that awful day that Ethan's life was taken. Surprisingly, the first person to arrive at my house, other than my sister and best friend, whom I had called, was the pastor from the church I had walked away from all those years earlier. Of course, he was Tom's pastor at that time, but I had no doubt when he arrived that he was there for me also.

Early the next morning when Tom and I and our son, Jeff, arrived in Mississippi to be with Ethan's wife and children, I lay wide awake in a darkened hotel room; I was in incredible pain. It was pain so deep, it was as physical as it was emotional. I cried out to God, never doubting He was there, but would He respond to someone who hadn't bothered to speak to Him for years? I think if He hadn't responded, I wouldn't have made it through that night or the extended period of intense grief that followed. Miraculously, God began to comfort and strengthen me within hours. I remember often, that same pastor who came to my house to comfort me, saying: *"God will never turn away from you. You may turn away from Him, but He will always be waiting for you to return."*

35

TILL I CAN MAKE IT ON MY OWN

*T*his song is about someone trying to stand on their own two feet, because a relationship has ended and the support the lost love gave is no longer available. As we mature, we are taught we should be as independent as we are capable of being. Even those who marry and go through life with a partner, are expected to exhibit a certain degree of independence in thought and action. Some people are physically incapable of being independent and some of us are emotionally incapable of independence. The world presents independence as a goal to be achieved along the path to success; as with much of the world's thinking, this is upside down.

God never intended for us to go it alone; our human journey was supposed to include Him. Our lives never go as well without His presence. Many people look at a relationship with God as unnecessary baggage; just one more thing that requires our attention or one more being with an expectation of what we should do or not do.

A true relationship with God isn't a burdensome thing; it's just the opposite. It's freedom from so many things that weigh us down; freedom from worry and fear; freedom from loneliness; freedom from doubt and guilt etc. That's a lot of baggage to carry around needlessly.

These things are only a burden to us if we don't give them to God, who wants to take care of them for us as only He can. What friend in this world would ask to do that much and who here could be relied upon to do it without failure and to carry such a weight for us for our entire lifetime?

One of the unforgettable thrills of parenthood, is teaching your child how to walk. We are so excited to see our babies take their first steps, without holding on to us; yet we stay nearby, ready to catch them if they fall. We pick them up, give them words of encouragement and let them try again. Even after they grow to adulthood and claim their independence by leaving our home to establish their own, we stand by, ready to be called on for support, encouragement, practical advice, sympathy and love. God the Father, does these things also, and so much more, but like an ideal human parent, He waits to be asked. He doesn't insert Himself, and try to dominate our lives without being asked to help. Most of us try to stay in close contact with our human parents; we don't all do nearly as well with our divine parent.

So many of us were taught that God is sitting on a throne somewhere up in the clouds, looking down at us wearing a look of displeasure and watching all the time to see what we're doing wrong. A relationship with God is about love and guidance; there is no scripture that says: *"God is judgement. I John:4 says:" God is Love"*. That means everything God does is from a spirit of love; His Spirit. It is very difficult as an adult to reject the things you were taught as a child, by those you love and trust. No one deliberately mislead you; it's more a matter of perspective. The Bible speaks truth, and each reader perceives it differently. It speaks to each individual spirit as that person is able to understand and receive it. That is what makes it the "Living Word of God". It isn't just words on paper; it's alive in every age of this world.

There is no need for you to try to make it on your own; God is constantly watchful, loving and tenderly compassionate in His desire to help us navigate the often difficult journey through this world. He's like any other parent; He's waiting for His children to come Home.

36

UNDUN/SHE'S COME UNDONE

*I*f you have never experienced a sudden horrific shock, you are probably unaware of the damage it can do to your central nervous system; this is apart from the emotional damage that can be ongoing. It has been a little over 5 yrs. since I lost my son and there are still lingering physical effects. I manage to maintain my emotional balance most of the time, through living a large portion of my life in the spiritual space I created for myself. But sometimes my equilibrium can be suddenly and easily upset by things I don't control or anticipate. These are outside stimuli, such as a sudden loud noise; I have developed a total aversion to fireworks! I can't watch suspenseful movies or anything violent. I can't listen to the sad old songs I've always loved. Anything unexpected jangles my nerves so badly, that I struggle for hours or even days to regain my equilibrium.

I struggle a lot with how much of the world outside my door, I am able to handle. It is so much easier and safer to live most of my time in my carefully controlled environment; my sanctuary. Why is that a struggle? Because I know we are meant to live our lives doing both of these things; usually in a much more balanced fashion.

The current degree of separation, due to Covid 19 isn't as much of a burden for me, as it is for many people, because I am most comfortable at home. The biggest hardship for me is not being able to spend time with my family. We don't visit in each other's homes at this point, when the virus is raging. We sit outside when weather permits, but now we are going into Winter and those opportunities will be fewer.

One of the reasons I see my hesitance to spend much time away from my own home as something to be concerned about, is that there is a tendency in my mother's family to self-isolate. Her half-sister suffered from agoraphobia and at times my mother seemed to be hampered by it as well. Aunt Mona became so fearful of leaving her home that she missed her children's graduations and weddings and near the end of her life she refused to leave home to be seen by a doctor, even though it might have given her more time.

In the early days of my grief, after losing Ethan, my memories brought me only pain, but after a few months they began to be a treasure to me and I was happiest living in the past. The past was less painful because it was a place I could go to and have all of my children. I thought perhaps, this was the way to live as I went forward with life, but then I received a message from Ethan in which he told me it was okay to enjoy the past, but I couldn't live my life there and I still had a life to live. I could see he was right; I still cherish my memories, but I know my life must be lived in the present.

I no longer live in fear, though I spent much of my life in that state. That changed in moments, as I looked deeply into Jesus eyes the day of Ethan's service. When I come "undone", it has nothing to do with being afraid, it is an involuntary response; a nervous system glitch. I have begun to believe this damage will be a permanent part of my life, but I try hard not to be crippled by it.

As a child, my brother and I would sometimes play at the city park. There were always other kids there and I remember one boy who liked to stand in the middle of the teeter totter and try to balance both ends as long as he could. He was never successful for very long; one end or the other would fall.

In my grief, I would tell my sister, that I felt like I was always trying to balance on a chair that only had three of it's four legs. That means you are never completely relaxed while you do this. I have learned to turn inside to the place where my spirit resides in peace and there, I find balance. These challenges are part of my life now and in spite of them, my life is good; it is blessed. I will never take that for granted; it's a miracle!

37

IT DON'T MATTER TO ME

*T*he son I lost, Ethan, was an historian; he studied the past with a great fascination for what it can reveal. Many people in my extended family look at it the same way Ethan did. For me, the past has always provided a sense of grounding or belonging. I am comforted by surrounding myself with things from years gone by. Most people today only want what's new. Nostalgia is clearly out of vogue; it seems to be disappearing from our lives. People spend most of their time looking for the next new thing.

The problem I see with always looking to the future, is that we fail to appreciate the moment we are in. Now is the only moment when heaven and earth intersect; knowing that and observing the "now" moment can have a great impact on how you live your life. After Ethan's life was taken, he encouraged me to not look too far into the future, but to get through each now moment. It made those awful days easier to live one moment at a time. Contemplating a future without my son, seemed unbearable at that point. None of us knows how long our future here could be; it might be shorter than you anticipate or maybe much longer. You are probably better off not to speculate.

Being more present in each moment gives me pause to reflect on how good my life is at any given time. I contemplate each blessing I receive; counting your blessings is a great way to stay in emotional and spiritual balance.

I am so enamored with the past; I have often wondered if I had somehow landed in the wrong time-period or if I lived a previous life in another time. Even the way I write and the words I use, reveal my obsession with the past.

I look at the world as it is today and it seems strange and unfamiliar to me; much of what I see disturbs me. I choose to spend a lot of my time in a kinder and gentler, much slower paced place; sometimes that place is the past and sometimes it is my spiritual place. These places both help me maintain my balance in this world gone mad. I can't remember the exact moment when I first looked at the world and found that I recognized very little of it. I know it was back a number of years; back before I lost Ethan. The murder of my son wasn't the catalyst for this kind of thinking; it was more like the final piece of evidence I needed to confirm the conclusion that the world had become a strange and hostile place for me. This world made no sense to me then and it still doesn't; for a long while I really felt it was important that it make sense. Now I know it really doesn't matter.

Many people believe that life on this planet is some kind of illusion; I've come to believe that is most likely the truth. My spiritual journey has reinforced the idea that "this world is not my home." In light of that, I choose to create for myself a world better suited to my consciousness and comfort, perhaps, that is my illusion; I think not! If you are thinking right now, that I've become mentally unbalanced, you couldn't be farther from the truth. I am a great deal more rational, and sane, than I have ever been. I have seen the truth and the truth has indeed, set me free. This truth has been revealed to me by the Holy Spirit and the illusion the world believes to be true, no longer interests me.

The world, collectively decides what has value and when something has lost its value. We follow along like a flock of sheep; why do we do this? Because they say we should? Who are "they" and who gave them this power over us? I don't believe the crazy thing is to question this unknown and unproven authority; I think it's the only intelligent and rational thing to do.

It became imperative that I follow the guidance of the Holy Spirit, as I tried to rebuild my shattered world after Ethan's life was taken. I have to maintain my peace in a kinder and more loving place than the great illusion provides.

I send you blessings whatever path you choose to follow, but please, let it be a path of your own choosing.

38

HAVE THINE OWN WAY

I have always found security and stability in things that were constant; I didn't like change and I didn't readily accept it. I preferred to live with something that was imperfect, rather than trust that the next unknown thing might be better; I always doubted that it would. It took many years for me to realize that my insistence on holding onto sameness, was also holding me back. It held me back in many aspects of life, but most importantly it held me back spiritually. You can't sail away if you refuse to pull up the anchor; your spirit can't soar if you keep it in a cage.

It isn't wrong to want or need to have an anchor, but mine was planted firmly in things of this world. It should have been planted in Jesus, the foundation, the rock. I only discovered my mistake when I lost my son; at that point I just surrendered; I had nothing left in me with which to fight. I knew if God didn't help me get through those agonizing days, I wouldn't continue to exist.

Surrender doesn't have to be as painful as the experience I had, but it often takes trauma, drama or desperation, to put us at the edge of the cliff, before we can see the need to ask for God's help.

Taking that one step toward God, changed my life dramatically. I didn't surrender my free-will; I surrendered my fear. I didn't surrender my self-determination; I just turned on a divine GPS. The imagery of that moment is similar to the Wizard of Oz's Dorothy opening the front door to the beauty and magic of Munchkinland. Everything became clearer and brighter and more colorful; suddenly everything was bathed in light. I had opened the door to the whole universe and it wasn't scary at all. I felt like I had finally let myself out of the box I had built to hide in.

There has never been a time since I relinquished my need to follow the path, I laid out for myself, that I have felt pushed or forced to do or be anything or anyone but myself. I'm just a better self; a truer self than I was before.

My need to have constancy in my life has been filled in the companionship of Jesus. I've seen Him and looked into His amazing eyes and He told me He is always with me. I feel that, as I have never been able to feel it before. It doesn't mean I will live a charmed life and never again feel pain, or loss or grief; it means that together Jesus and I will come out on the other side of these things. It is blessed assurance in an uncertain world.

39

FIVE MINUTES

I used to tell my children frequently: *"life requires patience."* We don't seem to be born with much patience. It was about twenty-five years before I could claim to be a patient person; it took losing my son to discover just how much patience life can demand of you and the true value of it.

Patience is something that has to grow within us and it grows like a tree; slowly. Impatiently, we want it to grow quickly; like a weed. If you've ever seen a flower bloom in time-lapse photography, you observe the entire process in a matter of seconds; while observing the same flower bloom in real time would likely take hours or even days. Everything that happens in nature, occurs in divine right time. Nature never gets in a hurry and it's never late. If our Spring flowers open up and then a frost comes and kills them, we say they bloomed too early; what actually happens is that because humans have been disturbing nature's natural rhythm and timing for centuries now, the frost came late.

You may remember a time when children were told to count to ten, before responding in anger to whatever had upset them. While that was a strategy to combat them lashing out or just being reactive to anger, it's also a strategy that could be used to teach patience. Reactivity is the opposite of patience; it is the epitome of the old saying "shoot first and ask questions later", not a workable philosophy in practical application.

Sooner or later, we are all faced with a situation that requires a much greater degree of patience than we can normally call forth; this is where real patience begins to grow and mature. Typically, we all have a greater degree of patience in certain areas than others. Some of us are quite patient with babies and small children. Some of us have more patience with our pets. Some of us have a great deal of patience when exercising our creativity, but less patience standing in line at the checkout, to pay for the supplies we need, in order to be creative. The fact is we generally decide what we will give a greater degree of patience to.

When I began the grieving process after losing my son, I often wanted those first few intensely painful weeks to pass more quickly. They had to be lived one moment at a time and every few minutes I would think "I just can't stand this another moment. If there was just someplace to go to get away from myself, it would help so much!" Of course, there was no place like that, so I had to learn to be patient with the process. I had to stop fighting with it and just let it take me where it would. As time passed, the pain didn't just go away, but it was transformed in subtle, yet important ways. The pain is still there and it will always be, but through the miraculous process of grief that God created, I have been able to transcend my pain and live joyously and hopefully, even knowing the pain will always be a part of my life in this place.

Following my 60th birthday, I suddenly realized I needed to slow everything down; I had no idea why, but I sensed it was important and it needed to happen. When I look around me at the people I know well; it doesn't seem to be something that happens in everyone's life. Perhaps, it is supposed to, but as with most things, maybe we are free to accept it or reject it as we wish.

We all seem to be in a hurry to arrive somewhere; that somewhere is a place unknown to us most of our lives. Then suddenly, we discover we are there; we've arrived at a place in life called maturity; a place of wisdom gained along the way to our journey's end. Suddenly, the angst and impatience is gone. As we realize we have more life behind us than ahead of us and that knowledge changes everything. Suddenly, we aren't in such a hurry; we want to savor as much of life as we can, like a delicious morsel.

Out of the blue, life has become somehow sweeter, even in light of the very bitter pills we may have been required to swallow along the way. We have fought through all of the seemingly insurmountable challenges and in spite of our missteps we have risen to the top, we stand on the summit of the great mountain and we realize how perfectly God has made us, how strong we have become, how fearlessly we walk into the wind and the rain. We realize, even with creaky joints and aching backs, how quickly we have learned to get up off of the floor when life knocks us to the ground. We know who we are, we know where we are bound, we know why we came. The secrets of life are no longer hidden and we no longer search impatiently. Eternity waits just beyond the horizon; God smiles and patiently waits for our return.

40

HOOKED ON A FEELING

*A*bout 25 yrs. ago, I decided to take a rug hooking class. I had always admired the beauty of hand hooked rugs and I love creating things with my own hands.

There happened to be a very skilled rug hooking teacher living in my hometown; her name was Virgie and at that time she was in her 90's. I enjoyed learning how to create the beautiful shaded flowers and leaves in the patterns, but I enjoyed Virgie even more. I decided after the first class that she was who I wanted to be when I was 90. She was always smiling, always cheerful and seemed to take everything in stride. She loved teaching people to make beautiful rugs and she loved hearing about the things her students did in other aspects of their lives. She had likely made hundreds of rugs over the years and hundreds of friends in the process; I'm sure she had one in progress when she passed away at 100 yrs. plus.

There were times when rug hooking class seemed like one more thing to do after a long tiring day, but I always went because I couldn't stand disappointing her. Once I got there and started working; I forgot all about being tired, my mood would lift and I felt reinvigorated when class was over.

Virgie's son was a teacher at the high school I attended

many years earlier and he talked about her often during the years I took his horticulture class. He loved to tell everyone his mother was the "oldest hooker" on the planet. He and his wife owned a sheep farm just outside my hometown and his wife learned to spin wool on an old-fashioned spinning wheel and how to color the wool using natural dyes from things that grew on their farm. She taught spinning and dying classes and between her and Virgie they could give you a start to finish course in sheep's wool.

Virgie's son was her only living child; her daughter passed away early in her adult life from cancer. Virgie found a way to enjoy life, in spite of her loss.

Life's troubles often have a way of robbing people of their enthusiasm for living and many times their worst tragedies live on in their personality and interactions with others. Virgie had found peace and her persistent smile and unfailing kindness gave her an inner glow it's rare to find in people. I want my own tragic loss to shine through me like a golden light; it isn't the loss I want people to see in me, but the light of heaven's healing and my deepening relationship with Jesus, who turns tragedy to triumph.

"O death, where is thy sting? O grave, where is thy victory?

1 Corinthians 15:55-57

41

OLD DOGS, CHILDREN, AND WATERMELON WINE

*Y*es, believe it or not, this chapter title is really a song; it couldn't be more perfect, because this chapter is about things that need to be nurtured. One of the definitions of nurturing is: to cherish; it's the definition I like best, because to cherish something means that it is a treasure in your life. Matthew 6:21 reads: *for where your treasure is, there your heart will be also.*

There are not many things in this world that we care deeply enough about to give our heart to them; our heart is our greatest treasure and most of us guard it zealously. The majority of us have no problem giving our heart totally to our children; many of us can give our heart to the children of the world, those not born of our own flesh and blood. As a parent, when your child dies, your heart is crushed and broken and that causes both physical and emotional pain. Without having a heart that can be broken, we are something less than human. Human beings are programmed to love some things and some people passionately. To do so, is to risk all that you are spiritually. Your spirit can't be destroyed, but it can be severely damaged. Many people fear giving their heart, and therefore themselves, completely; it is what real true love requires. When you can't or won't give love completely, you can't receive love completely. This is why the old saying: *"it is better to give than to receive"*, makes sense, because giving is the key to receiving.

Children are so easy to love; they respond to love with such innocence and so little judgement or expectation. Many parents who didn't feel loved as children, find it harder to give themselves completely to their own offspring.

As a child, I often felt unloved; I wasn't unloved, I just felt that way. When you feel unloved you begin to believe it's because you are unlovable or undeserving of being loved. You begin to believe there is something wrong with you. My parents loved me and they thought I should know that, without them saying it was so. They were a product of their own home environments. When they were children, people were not as openly affectionate as they are now. My father used to tell me: *"You should know I love you, by the things I do for you."* In my case, that didn't seem to be enough.

When I had my own children, I wanted them to know I loved them, without question. Because I reached a point in my own life, where I seriously considered suicide, I never wanted my children to reach that dark place and not be able to say: *"but my mother loves me!"*

I hoped that would be enough to make them reconsider taking their own lives. They were the only reason I didn't take mine. I told them I loved them every day. I said it so often they probably got sick of hearing it. I guess I sort of approached it like brain-washing. I wanted that thought to be able to float to the surface easily; especially in times of despair or desperation. None of us can truly know how deeply another person feels negative emotions. We are always shocked, dismayed and often surprised when someone we know and thought was doing well, suddenly ends their own life.

Our society believes we cease to be children when we
turn 18 yrs. old, as if that number magically erases all of the
insecurities of childhood and they are forbidden to play a role
in our adult life. Somewhere inside of us, the child we were still
exists, still needing to be cherished and nurtured. Many people
believe that nurturing yourself is an indication of narcissism.
The truth is, being able to nurture yourself, your inner child,
is a completely different thing than feeding your adult ego. If
we truly love others, we should be able to see and support the
child still living within them.

My husband and I now live in a town where, we suspect,
dogs outnumber people by at least a 2:1 ratio. Observing
the behavior of people with their dogs, is very similar to
observing parents with their children. There are those who are
completely oblivious to the ridiculous behaviors they exhibit
while trying to please their four-legged loved ones. Then there
are those who's pets are placed in a pen, fed, watered and
virtually ignored. Being able or unable to love and nurture a
pet, says a lot about you and your ability to love and nurture
other human beings. Some people want a pet to be a loving
companion, some people want a dog to be a protector, some
people want a dog as disagreeable as they are, because it
supports their right to be so, some people want a dog because
everyone else has one or two or three...

I have always been more of a cat person. I've had some really
frightening experiences with dogs, in the past and I'm still
very uncomfortable around dogs I haven't been around a lot
or who's owners aren't close by. I have been the owner of two
dogs, one experience was really bad and shameful; the other
experience taught me a lot about my- self and how much love
animals are capable of giving unconditionally.

Here is my story of shame: Right after Tom and I were

married and while we were trying to figure out how to become a family with my two children, my supervisor at work wanted me to take a dog that needed a new home. It was a very cute little dog and had been a much loved family pet. The owners were moving and could no longer keep it. They wanted to find a good home for it. I was newly married, had two young children and was expecting another; my plate was quite full at that point. My supervisor would not take no for an answer, even after I told her I was afraid of dogs, didn't know how to take care of a dog and didn't have the time or money to care for one. I still ended up with the dog. It was a dog, that today I would be delighted to have. We put it in a pen in the back yard and other than food and water, no one paid attention to it. Things got so bad, we eventually took it to a shelter, where I pray it found the good home and family it deserved. This is an episode in my life that fills me with shame and regret to this day. I try not to think about it, but I hope at least in sharing it, a greater purpose will be served.

About 8 yrs. later, my sister, Jeanne, wanted me to go with her to see some puppies that her neighbors were selling. Since I was the person who had unfortunately run over the dog her children had grown up with; I hated to refuse to go with her. Not only did she find a dog, she talked me into getting a puppy and aside from being astonished to have taken one home, I even paid $200 for it. My sister often has this effect on me; don't ask me how she does it!

The puppy was so small, it would nearly fit into a teacup. With Jeanne's help and guidance, I set about learning how to take care of it. I named her Ginger, because of the color of her coat; she was a Lhasa Apso; if you look up the temperament of this breed you find they are devoted, intelligent, fearless, spirited and playful. She was all of that and she became my companion and friend. My family claimed to only tolerate her, but I think they really loved her. The problem was, like a lot of small breed dogs, she was a one-person pet. She loved me; she was bit suspicious of everyone else. We had her a little over 10 yrs. and when the time came that putting her to sleep was the humane thing to do, I was devastated; I cried for a solid week. My husband has never gotten over taking her that day and since then refuses to have another dog. Nearly 45 yrs. later, I still have a little bag of Ginger's toys in my cedar chest and I just can't let them go. It still hurts my heart to be without her.

The watermelon wine part of this story is actually about growing things. I've never grown watermelons, but I have no doubt that I could. My great love is growing plants and flowers. When you see someone, who has a "green thumb" as they say, you are really seeing someone who has a nurturing spirit toward things that grow. Just as you have to learn to care for a child or a pet, you have to learn to take care of things that grow. They respond to nurturing. Every living thing God created has His spirit within it and responds to being cherished. I'm not sure about snakes, spiders and mosquitos, but maybe I'm just not there yet.

It is so important to love and be loved and that is the message this chapter is meant to share. I want that message to resonate with every single person who reads my books. It's the reason I need to write in the first place.

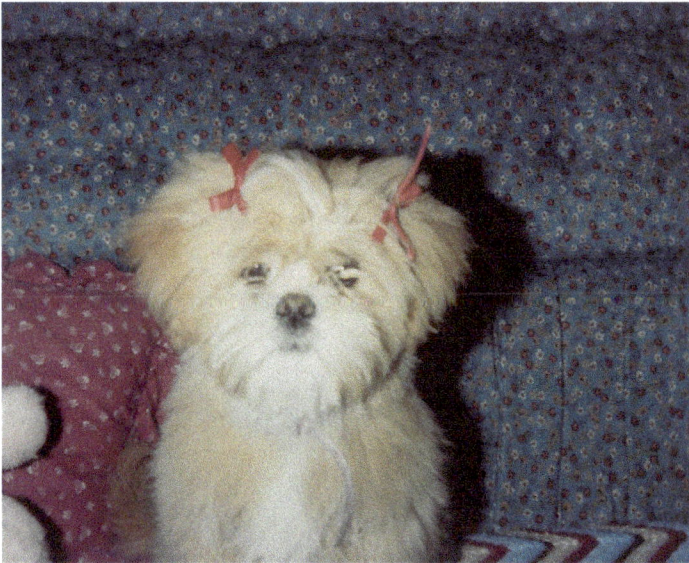

My sweet Ginger.

42

SWEET HOUR OF PRAYER

*I*t is my personal observation that human beings do not respond positively to negative messaging. I think this is particularly true regarding spiritual things.

Many years ago, I had a friend who regularly sent her children to one of the local churches, on Sunday morning to attend Sunday School; she and her husband did not attend. He was christened a Catholic and had not practiced that faith since childhood. He carried with him memories of a tough childhood and foster parents who neglected and abused him; all while professing their Catholic faith.

One day, I was visiting my friend and the doorbell rang. She went to the door and opened it; the person outside, rudely and forcefully pushed her way in, not waiting to be invited to enter. It was an older woman from the church where my friend's children attended. She pointed her finger at their father and announced: *"You're going to hell! If you ever set foot in a church the roof would fall in!"*

Needless to say, her overzealous, but good intentions had the opposite effect of the one she intended. It was decades before my friend's husband began attending another local church. That happened because the pastor of that church made friends with him at the local café over coffee. The pastor treated him no differently than he would have treated any member of his congregation.

Over the years, I have answered my door numerous times to find a pair of fresh-faced, overdressed young people, Bibles in hand, who announced they had come to inform me about God. I would politely explain that I had grown up in church; my father and several grandfathers had been ministers, etc. They kept right on talking as though I'd said nothing. Then, I explained I was a long- time member and fundraising chairman of a local church. They kept on talking and I would get extremely annoyed by their presumption that I knew nothing of God. I would eventually mutter a quick excuse and shut the door; they would still be talking. I hate rudeness and I hate being put in a position that forces me to be so. Many people consider what these people do to be witnessing. I do not; I believe God provides many opportunities for us to witness to others in a more natural and welcome way. The key is to wait, watch for, and be open to these occasions and be willing to act on them when the time is right.

I find the messages coming from the pulpits of many established churches to be extremely negative. That puzzles me exceedingly because Jesus message is one of love, hope, compassion and forgiveness. I don't think very many people respond well to being told God is mad at them and looking to exact revenge on everyone who doesn't believe as they and their church do. I also don't believe the first question upon arrival in the next life will be: *"What church do you attend?"*

If you're beginning to think I'm antichurch, you're mistaken. Churches serve a very necessary purpose for many people; but if you go there thinking it's the place to find and establish your own personal relationship with God, you will likely be disappointed. Most churches serve to help support you in your faith and being with like minded people can certainly do that. They can also provide social activities that do not conflict with your growing faith, something that's hard to find in the opportunities presented by the world at large. I believe the negativity many churches project in their representation of the "Gospel of Jesus; the Good News", may be the reason fewer and fewer people are attending church.

A few years ago, my husband and I attended a gospel concert given by a group whose music I found soothed my spirit tremendously in my time of grief. It took place at a Christian College near where we live. As soon as we were seated, an elderly man leaned forward in his seat and asked if we were members of the same religious organization that the performers were. When I answered that we weren't; his smile instantly changed to a look of sheer revulsion and he shrank back in his seat. I actually thought he would move to another seat because he was so upset with my answer.

I believe true "witnessing" is in the observance of others of someone who "lives" their faith every day in as many ways as possible. None of us will ever be perfect and no one here has a right to expect us to be so, but Jesus said we were to strive for the greatest degree of perfection we could attain. I don't believe that is what will make us acceptable; we are made acceptable through Jesus death and resurrection. Jesus didn't say we should go around looking down our noses at people who don't go to our church. He told us to be humble and kind to others. He said to pray for each other and love each other. Jesus doesn't need us to try to change someone else's behavior in any other way except by the expression of faith that radiates from our spirit into the world.

43

HOW WILL I KNOW?

*W*hen we think about having an impact on someone's life, we usually think about something big and obvious, but I don't think it happens that way very often. Most of the time it's something more obscure and possibly hard to recognize at the time. I can think of several times when someone impacted my life in a positive way that I've never forgotten, but I'm sure they never knew it.

I've previously written about a man I knew, who convinced me that I was destined to only give birth to male children. During the time my first marriage was ending, and not ending easily or painlessly, my estranged husband, who didn't want a divorce, began to play some devious and spiteful mind games. There was so much drama in my life, I thought I was going crazy. The man, I mentioned, told me one day: *"You're a lot stronger than you think you are. Why do you let him manipulate you; he can't do that unless you let him."* Those two statements changed everything for me; I knew that was true, but I needed to hear someone else say it. I have always been rather amazed that during that painful time, when a man was the source of my pain and confusion, the very best advice I got didn't come from my female friends; it came from men.

I had another friend, who happened to be a former classmate of my Mother's, who asked me one day, if I was going to get a divorce? I said I was only going to get a legal separation. He then asked me: *"Is there any way this marriage can be saved?"* My answer was no, and he said: *"In that case, what you need is a divorce."* Hearing someone else put that into words, made it clear in my own mind and I was able to move forward in a way that was really going to change my life for the better; instead of just prolonging the inevitable.

I've written elsewhere, about my friend, Raven, who demonstrated by her own life, that failure wasn't the worst thing that could happen to you. I watched her closely and learned a lot. I had more confidence and success, once I learned not to fear failure, but to use it as a step to propel myself forward and reach my objectives.

These are just a few examples, that I believe, prove that each person whose life intersects with your own, has something to teach you and you will likely never know what it is or when the lesson was learned. In many of the books I've read, the planet we live on is referred to as the "Earth school". We come here to learn a lot more than Reading, Writing and Arithmetic.

44

LAUGHING

Many people my age will remember the great, Erma Bombeck; what made her great, you ask? She made us laugh; we laughed at her; with her and she taught us to laugh at ourselves and at life. She was more than a comedian; she was a humorist. A comedian makes us laugh by delivering a punchline; a humorist uses wit, intellect and the written word to convey humor and so much more. Just getting us to laugh isn't their objective; they want to make us think. When you look up Erma Bombeck online; you find her mentioned in the company of such great humorists as Mark Twain, Will Rogers and Benjamin Franklin.

Erma wrote a syndicated newspaper column from 1965-1996; she also published 15 books. Her writing chronicled the ordinary life of a midwestern housewife. In actual fact, she had little to laugh about; she was diagnosed with a genetic kidney condition at the age of 20. She suffered a bout with breast cancer and the resulting mastectomy. She endured years of daily dialysis for her kidney ailment and passed at the age of 69. Laughter was her way of coping with pain and illness. She taught us not to take life too seriously and to enjoy the ride; even when things weren't so great.

There are many clichés about laughter; the one that comes to mind first is: "Laughter is the best medicine." There are actually scientific studies to prove the truth of that statement. Here are a couple more, I think are great: "Laughter is timeless, imagination has no age, and dreams are forever". That one is from Walt Disney. Bob Hope said this:" I have seen what laughter can do. It can transform almost unbearable tears into something bearable, and even hopeful".

After my mother's passing, one of the things I missed most about her was her sense of humor. Sometimes; a lot of times, it was a bit off-color, but just watching her enjoy something funny or ridiculous made you feel good. She would sometimes call me to tell me something she'd read or seen or thought of herself that she found humorous. I would answer the phone and there would only be the faint sound of someone laughing so hard they couldn't talk. I knew immediately, it was Mother.

She loved to laugh and worked hard at finding humor in her life. She had an unhappy childhood and whenever she felt a bit blue; she would find something to laugh about and lift her spirits. She loved to tell jokes and funny stories; she loved to sing silly songs. I used to find some of these things embarrassing, as a teenager. After she was gone, I finally understood why it was so important for her to find something to laugh about; I realized that quirky sense of humor was one of the things that made her unique.

My father had a sister, whose name was Juanita; we called her Aunt Nita. She passed away several years ago; when I think of her I remember her laughter. She also had a tough life, but she loved to laugh. I always enjoyed seeing her put her whole self into it; she would throw her head back, slap her leg and rock back and forth. She had so little to laugh about; there was a lot of cruelty in her life, but she found reasons to laugh.

I remember Ethan laughing too. I loved the way it sounded; it's one of the things I miss most. Ethan loved life and he laughed a lot. When he was taken from us, I wasn't sure I would ever laugh again and I was shocked the first time it happened. Ethan tells me often, he wants us to enjoy our lives and really live them fully and with meaning. When we laugh, his spirit is very close to us.

When we are able to laugh, in spite of our pain and loss, it is a spiritual victory. Laughter helps piece the broken parts of us back together; that is a gift from God. We need to be made whole again and when we learn the value of laughter through pain; laughter at ourselves and with others, we truly begin to understand what a wondrous gift life is.

45

STANDING ON THE PROMISES

Much of my life I lived in fear, not the overwhelming kind of fear that prevents you from living a "normal" life; whatever normal is? I lived with a lot of little gnawing fears; the kind you can usually hide from other people, but they have a tremendous impact on your ability to really live life to its fullest measure.

The one that comes to mind first, is failure; failure of any kind, for any reason. I came to believe that the most certain way to avoid failure, was simply not to try to do anything if I didn't feel certain of the outcome. That kind of thinking leaves you fenced into a pretty small space. I fenced out a lot of possibilities for myself. It felt much safer to keep my world small and manageable.

I did just that until I was about 30 yrs. old; then I met someone who unknowingly changed my life. I've written about her before and I felt compelled to give her a fictitious name in order to protect her identity; I call her Raven. She passed away at the age of 29. I only knew her for a little over a year, yet she had a lasting impact on my life. As I look back on my brief relationship with Raven, I know we were destined to meet, because she had something important to teach me.

The thing about Raven that touched me in such a lasting way, was that she appeared to be fearless. What I mean is that she wasn't afraid of failure. She was an artist with an artist's way of viewing the world. Artists often have many rejected attempts when trying to create what they see in their minds eye. They don't see those attempts as failures; they see them as necessary steps in their creative process.

I am also a very creative person, but I never saw failure in that way, until I observed the way Raven took it in stride. Becoming who you were meant to be is a process and all of us suffer many failures along the way. There is an old saying: *"When one door closes another door opens".* If you just stand and stare at the door that is closed, you will never see the one that is newly opened.

I spent a lot of time obsessing about my failures. That time would have been better spent assessing them to figure out how to turn them into successes. Raven had no time for looking back; perhaps, she knew somehow her time her was short. She always sought another way to accomplish what she wanted to do.

In getting to know her and watch her in action, I came to realize failure wasn't the disaster I had always believed it to be, and it doesn't get the last word unless you let it. When that happened, my fear of failure receded and it opened up a new world for me. My insecurities no longer had the power they once did to hold me back. My confidence in myself and my abilities to do many things began to blossom. I began to recognize unlimited possibilities and my creativity was free of the shackles that had suppressed it at last. I experienced tremendous personal growth just from observing someone else's ability to see failure as a tool for learning.

I spent nearly twenty years of my life as a professional

seamstress. I made nearly everything it is possible to make with fabric. The most high-pressure thing I made was wedding gowns. There is a lot of stress involved there because you have limited time, you are working with expensive materials and the expectation is very high that you are going to create a gown that fulfills someone's vision of the perfect dress, for their long-imagined perfect wedding.

I made wedding gowns for two of my daughters-in-law and it was an honor to get to do that for them. I made the first of those two dresses for my son Jeff's bride, Carol. When making wedding gowns, you always want to cut the entire dress from a single length of fabric, because there are way more color variations of white than you would ever imagine. I made a mistake when I cut the back of the skirt for Carol's dress and I didn't have enough fabric to recut that piece. I had to figure out what to do that would disguise the fact that I had made a mistake; it forced me to think more creatively. The solution I settled on gave the dress a more unique and lovelier train than it would have had if I'd cut it correctly. I was able to turn a failure into a triumph and I have to tell you that's a great feeling.

When you begin to listen for heaven's guidance, you come to realize God is not counting your failures; He's encouraging you to seek another path. If you hold your head up and look around, you can see the other path He's providing for you.

"Trust in the Lord with all your heart, and do not lean on your own understanding. In all your ways acknowledge Him, and He will make straight your paths."

Proverbs 3:5-6

"Standing on the promises, I cannot fail"

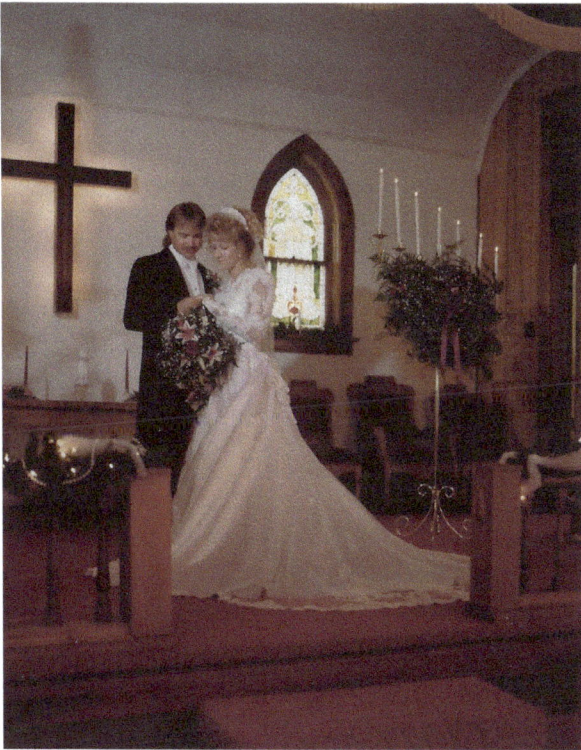

Jeff and Carol on their wedding day.

46

HOW DEEP IS YOUR LOVE?

*L*ove is such a small word, but such a big emotion. I'm talking about real love, the kind that transcends this world and goes with you into the next. This kind of love, is perhaps, God's most magnificent gift. I believe this kind of love is intended for all of us; how sad it is then, that so few ever find it.

This love I speak of here, is sweet and pure; it is beyond the pettiness and immature emotion the world defines as love. It is like water from the deepest natural spring; so deep it reaches to the very center of the Earth. It can't be polluted, or tarnished, or casually discarded. Once it is born, it exists eternally.

Perhaps, so few find it, because we look for it in the wrong places. It isn't somewhere out there; it lives deep inside us in the rhythm of our beating hearts. It is the song of our spirit; implanted by the Creator of love; God himself. It is the secret of life, the buried treasure, the sweetest song, the gold waiting at the end of the rainbow, the beauty in the tiniest snowflake, the majesty of an eagle in flight, the softness of a dove's coo, the joy in your heart when you look into the eyes of your newborn child, it is the sunset that leaves you breathless, it is the glory of a starlit sky, it is the flawless movement of a horse at full gallop, it is the thrill of dolphins leaping from the glassy surface of the ocean, it is as regal as a lion, as gentle as a lamb, as brilliant as a sparkling gem, as fragrant as the petal of a rose, as heartwarming as weathered hands that held each other from youth to death, and beyond. It is the pure essence of God.

When Ethan began to speak to me after his passing, his messages were all about love. He said to me many times: *"In the end, there is only love."* 1st Corinthians, chapter 13, is all about love and it ends with this: *"And now abide faith, hope, love, these three; but the greatest of these is love."*

When I saw the transfiguration of Jesus, on the day of Ethan's service, His whole presence shone with love and compassion. John 15:13 reads: *"Greater love hath no man than this, that he lay down his life for another."* The Bible tells us that is what Jesus did and when I looked into His eyes, I saw the depth of His love and I was transformed by it. Love is the energy of creation and it is always evolving. Never is there a point when there is "enough" love; that isn't possible. Love is a living, growing, changing thing. Love created every living thing that ever has or ever will exist. Love can only build; it cannot destroy. Love is life; love is expression; Love is God.

"I am the Alpha and the Omega; the first and the last, the beginning and the end.
Hebrews 11:10

47

THE IMPOSSIBLE DREAM

I was 12 yrs. old, when President Kennedy was assassinated; with his passing the world became a darker and sadder place. He was an idealist, a man who had the courage and insight to dream a huge dream.

An ideal is defined as a lofty goal; something it is unrealistic to believe can be achieved. It is a higher aspiration than a realist believes can be attained. It isn't that an idealist fully believes they can reach the unreachable goal; it's that they are willing to try anyway. President Kennedy inspired us to reach higher, work harder, dream bigger, and create things never before imagined.

His administration came to be known as "Camelot"; a place of legend, the castle of King Arthur and the location of the Knights of the Roundtable. King Arthur's knights each swore The Oath of Chivalry, which bound them to these ideals: Respect the honor of women, live by honor and for glory, protect the weak and defenseless, serve the King in valor and faith, love and honor God and His church.

The greatest knight in King Arthur's fictional realm was Sir Lancelot. He was believed to personify the Oath of Chivalry, but then he fell in love with the wife of the King and his betrayal led to the destruction of Camelot.

In the years since President Kennedy died, we have been inundated with books and documentaries detailing the truth of what lay behind the shining exterior of the modern- day Camelot. Our inspiring young hero was a flawed human being; as all human beings are. Why are so many of us shocked when we discover human beings are human, with human frailties?

So, once we know that this person (any person), who aspired to greatness and inspired us to be better, was imperfect, does that mean we should ignore or forget what he inspired us to do and become? I don't believe it does. Human beings don't put themselves on pedestals; we do that ourselves and many of us enjoy watching them rise and then we enjoy seeing them fall; our own human frailty, rearing its ugly head.

God has frequently chosen imperfect people for great assignments. If He chose only those who were close to perfection, there might be some question as to whether their accomplishment was their own, or if it was divinely guided.

King David was one of the most admired rulers in the Bible; he was anointed by God to lead the people of Israel. He inspired others to live and think on a higher level. He was a great leader and warrior, who successfully defended his people from many foes, but he was also a flawed human being. He saw the gravity of the mistakes he had made and sought forgiveness; it was granted him, but there was still a price to be paid; a very dear price. He is still honored today as one of the greatest leaders of his people.

There is no one on earth who can live up to life "on a pedestal". In today's world that pedestal is often great wealth or celebrity and many people take a very public fall from grace (the grace offered by humans). It is not ours to know or say, if they fall from God's grace.

We are all flawed, we are all learning to live in a world of changing values and unpredictable outcomes. Many people try to live and be the best they can be, but even though we strive with all that we are, we can never reach as high as God alone can lift us. Still we must try!

48

LEMON TREE

Many people believe that music is merely to entertain us, but it can also stir our emotions in a variety of ways. In addition to those two things, it often imparts wisdom, sometimes in the form of a thought- provoking lesson about life. "Lemon Tree" is a song about life; it is sometimes sweet and sometimes very bitter. People are not always who they appear to be; they nearly always are more complicated than they at first appear. Many situations in life begin sweetly, but after a time begin to grow sour.

When I was pregnant with my oldest son, I had an intense craving for lemons; I'd cut them in half and dip them in sugar. I can't even guess how many lemons I ate that way before my son was born. I was blessed to give birth to a very sweet little boy, in spite of all of the lemons I consumed. I mention this anecdote because I think it's human nature to sugarcoat things to make them seem more palatable to us. As I look back at my own life, I know I was pretty good at sugarcoating things. It never occurred to me when I was younger, that if something was in need of a coat of sugar to be acceptable, the best thing wasn't to try to hide it, but to change it. Things can often be easily changed, people cannot.

I learned that lesson eventually, but it took years of trying to change other people, before I realized it's actually easier to "exchange" people than it is to change them. You really only have the power to change yourself.

In my younger days, I was constantly devising some scheme to try to manipulate a situation, or the people within the situation to make it more to my liking. My plans almost always failed and you would think that would have been a good incentive to stop doing it. Instead of learning from those failures, I would just try a different tactic to achieve the result I was looking for. The person I needed to change was me. It took a lot of years and a lot of failure before I accepted that fact.

On the other hand, there's an old saying that goes "When life gives you lemons, make lemonade." I'm not sure that life is always responsible for the lemons we experience on our path; sometimes we pick them ourselves. When things seem to consistently turn sour, maybe it isn't a change of fruit or a spoonful of sugar that's needed.

Many of us have owned a vehicle at some point in life, that we considered to be "a lemon". It was constantly needing repairs and couldn't be relied on to get us to our destination. Lemons are yellow and sugarcoating them doesn't change the fact that they are lemons. If you painted your unreliable vehicle another color, or had the seats reupholstered, or tinted the windows, it would still be a lemon; real change has to occur from the inside out.

For many years, I avoided looking inside myself, because I was pretty sure I wouldn't like what I saw there. It didn't occur to me to change myself; I was always trying to change my circumstances, instead.
Our outward behavior often belies a restlessness or dissatisfaction on the inside and it's impossible to change

inwardly, if you never look there to identify the real problem. Introspection can take a long time and many people aren't interested in devoting that much focus in order to really come to know their true self. On the one hand, I could say I believe each of us is as God created us to be, and that would be true, but there is a best version of each of us and I believe we are supposed to be trying to achieve that best self, in the time we are given here.

49

HARD DAY'S NIGHT

God has blessed me in so many ways, yet there are times when the weight of the loss I carry threatens to pull me under. Jesus is always with me and He helps me maintain my balance when I begin to weaken and stagger a little.

These days it is not only the loss of my child that threatens to weigh me down, it is the chaos and uncertainty of the times we are living in, that adds so much to my burden. It is the negativity and the prejudice and the hate and disregard for human life, the lack of empathy and so much more.

Jesus is my strength and my comforter in times like these. He helps me carry my heavy load; He gives me strength when mine is failing. The world needs Jesus desperately, perhaps more than it ever has. I need Jesus every minute of my life; as I have never needed Him before. He is the light in the vast darkness that tries to cover all the Earth. I want His radiant illumination to shine within me to light my way but also to light the way of all who cross paths with me. Jesus' light and comfort are mine, whenever my thoughts gravitate to Him.

In six days, the anniversary of our tremendous loss, will again dawn. It has been 5 years since our lives exploded in anguish and pain. As that day approaches each year, I become very emotional. I begin to feel it building about two weeks before and even with Jesus to hold my hand, the tears and the ache to see my son return. I know the day will pass and I will regain my balance and composure, with Jesus help. He understands the depth of the loss I feel and doesn't see my fresh grief as a failing, or as ingratitude for all I have received through Him. I know He will always offer His hand to me in the hard moments of my life. He will always walk beside me through the darkness and into the light; He always brings the light.

"Then Jesus spoke to them again, saying: I am the light of the world. He who follows me shall not walk in darkness, but have the light of life."

50

LAUGH, LAUGH

Each of us sometimes says the wrong thing; maybe it's not really wrong, but it's misunderstood. Maybe our intention is good, but it just doesn't land on the person who hears it, in the way we meant it. I try never to hurt other people deliberately, but I admit to having done it. The new me always makes the effort to apologize; I want to be a support and encouragement to others.

Years ago, I served on a community board, with a woman I'll call Jane. I didn't know her well and our personalities tended to clash. We didn't argue, we just seemed to misunderstand each other easily.

There came a time when Jane discovered her husband was having an affair with his secretary; she was, of course, very angry and her heart was broken. She felt betrayed and decided to pursue a divorce. I had lived what she was feeling and I wanted to say something that would help her; what I said didn't help in the least! She thought it was insensitive and I didn't get a chance to finish what I was saying before she erupted. I understand her reaction and should have chosen my words much more carefully. Here's what I said: *"Well Jane, you have to laugh."* Sounds pretty bad doesn't it? What I was trying to get out was, if things get so bad that you can't find any humor in them at all, you're treading on dangerous ground. I have also lived that scenario!

She was so angry that I just let it drop without further attempts to explain what I meant. It really bothered me that she thought I was that insensitive and I tried to think of some way to calm the waters. After months and months of stress and misery, Jane decided to try to repair the damage to her marriage.

I was co-owner of a small antique and flea market business at that time and one day, Jane came in to buy something and I was the only person there. I took the opportunity to apologize and explain to her what I meant and that I knew the pain and humiliation she had suffered. At last, she understood that I hadn't meant to hurt her and I had freed myself from the guilt of having inadvertently done so. About two years later, Jane passed away from cancer. I was so relieved that I had made the effort to resolve the misunderstanding between us. You never know what will be your last opportunity to do the right thing; sooner is always better than later.

I once went to Texas with my parents to visit my maternal grandmother. She wanted us to help her pre-plan her funeral, because she didn't want anyone else to have to do it or pay for it. We went with her to the mortuary and listened as she declared what she wanted and didn't want to have happen. When we went to the casket showroom to make her selection, my Mother was just over whelmed with the sadness and morbidity of the whole episode and decided a little humor was in order. She asked my Grandmother if she would like for her to lay down in the casket she was considering, so Grandma could see what she would look like in it. I was horrified, but Grandma and my Mother both started giggling uncontrollably.

Then I was horrified because they were giggling. I'm sure the people at the mortuary had rarely, if ever, heard that sound coming from the casket showroom! My mother couldn't stand to think of losing her mother and it was her way of lightning the somber mood; inappropriate perhaps, but effective.

Sometimes, emotions can just get too over powering and laughter is like the safety valve on the pressure cooker. Laughter is every bit as necessary to our emotional health as tears are. After I lost my son, I couldn't imagine how I would ever laugh again; it took quite a while, and the first time it happened, it startled me. Ethan loved to laugh; I loved to hear him laugh and I know he wants me to find as much to laugh about as I can. There is a picture of Ethan, that I love, on the side of my refrigerator; I see it all the time. He is laughing; I remember the moment it was taken and I can almost hear the sound of his laughter each time I see it. That warms my heart!

Me and Grandma Tarpley (Big Marie).

51

CRYING

*I*f you have previously read any, or all of the books I've written, you may be thinking I'm obsessed with grief and spend my whole life in sadness and tears. That isn't really true; there are still some tears, sometimes there are tears every day, but those are only brief episodes and they go as quickly as they come. Yes, I cry, but I am blessed. Yes, my son was murdered, but I am blessed; I am not blessed because he was murdered, but in spite of what happened to him. He is still as gone from my life as he was in those first painful moments after I learned of the shocking tragedy that took him from us, but I am blessed. I will never again in this life, see his face or hear him laugh, or open my front door and see him standing there, but I am so richly blessed. My heart is still broken, God has mended it, but it will never be as it was; in spite of this, I am blessed. I miss my son every moment of every day, but I am so blessed to be able to feel his spirit near me and hear him speak to my heart; I am richly and abundantly blessed. I look in the mirror every day and I don't see the woman I was before that awful day; I see a woman that pain and loss aged almost instantly, but it doesn't matter. I am blessed. Yes, the life I knew and loved is gone forever, but I am blessed with a new life, a very similar life, yet not the same. It is a life I can live in peace, hope and joy, because God has given me courage and strength to bear what I could not bear alone. I am blessed beyond my ability to express it in words. I can never have the thing my heart wants most, but I am blessed beyond measure.

I have been touched by angels and I am blessed. I have heard the voice of the Holy Spirit and I am abundantly blessed. I have looked into the eyes of Jesus and I am astonished and humbled and amazingly blessed. I have received a calling to share my story of loss and healing with others, through speaking and writing and each time I can do that I am blessed. God allows me to feel my pain and loss and yet my tears are mingled with joy and peace and I am forever blessed.

52

PEACE TRAIN

*W*hat does it mean to have peace? I talk about peace in my spirit a lot; but if you have never had this kind of peace, it's hard to understand what it is and what it does for you.

As I often do when I write, I looked up the definition of peace, just to see how it compared to my own. It read: freedom from disturbance; tranquility. I don't entirely agree with that definition, but I understand it applies to human beings in a worldly sense; the peace I am talking about is spiritual.

Spiritual peace differs in some significant ways from the temporary kind of peace the world offers; once you have it, it is embedded so deeply into your spirit that I'm not sure it could ever leave you. I know it can't be taken from you against your will. You would have to relinquish it yourself and why would anyone ever do that?

To have this kind of peace is to feel God's presence deep inside you and know it will always be there no matter what kind of trouble or tragedy could be lurking just ahead of you. This peace is strength that you know is not your own, it is comfort from a source not of this world. It is to feel the presence of a constant companion and know you will never again feel alone or abandoned. It is to feel courage and hope, when there is much to be apprehensive of and you see little hope in the world around you.

This peace does not prevent you from experiencing pain or grief or anxiety, or any other human emotion; it simply supports you through them and lessens their ability to crush your spirit. The world we live in can be a difficult and dangerous place, but we have not been left in it without tools to help us find our way.

So, what are these tools, you might ask? How do I get them, where do I look for them? In Luke 17:21 Jesus said: *"The Kingdom of God is within you"*. The place to seek it is within yourself; it isn't "out there" somewhere.

If you are a living, breathing human being, you are a child of God; you could not exist otherwise. The presence of God is inside you, even when it goes unrecognized by you. You can deny God's presence; you can do all you can to eradicate it, but it will still be there.

Finding spiritual peace is just a matter of becoming conscious of it and holding it in your heart. I lived most of my life without feeling God's presence within. It was only when I sought God's comfort in the darkness of grief, that I discovered His presence inside myself. When I completely surrendered my self-determination and admitted that without Him, I couldn't go on, I began to feel Him in the empty place inside that I had never before understood.

I always knew that empty place was there, but I never understood why it was there, or how it could be filled. Having it filled with God's presence, is like suddenly discovering you have an additional internal organ that's just been activated and that makes your whole life finally make sense.

To seek God's presence outside of yourself, even in a church is not really the way to secure it. God exists everywhere; He's present in a church, but just being there won't create the personal, intimate relationship with Him that leads to His perfect peace. That place must be sought on a personal level, usually in a private place, one on one.

Once you discover this peace within, you realize that it's value cannot be described with mere words. There is no more priceless or miraculous thing in this world and you wonder why it isn't sought after like the most precious treasure. Many people go through the motions of seeking it, but that would be like searching the world for buried treasure, standing over the spot where you know it is and refusing to dig for it. Few of us would do that.

God hasn't buried His treasure in some remote and inaccessible place; it's buried inside you; all you have to do is look for it there.

I remember as a very small child, wondering how I got here and where had I come from. I had no answers to those questions that repeatedly popped into my mind, over the course of my life. Then suddenly, in the midst of my search for truth, comfort and peace, I began to see the Truth about my life. Over these past 5 yrs. since my son passed, I have learned to discern the truth; spiritual Truth; the only kind that really matters.

One of the things I know, is that I came from God and I will return to God. Another thing I know is that God put me in exactly the right place; even though I spent many years feeling like I wasn't living in the right place or the right time. I know now that I was destined to meet every single person whose life has intersected with mine, even if only momentarily. I was meant to experience everything that has happened, even the worst of it; the mistakes, the wrong marriage and subsequent divorce, the pain and loss, the joy and contentment. I was put here to experience love and loss.

Only recently, have I begun to realize that I have reached a point when it is time to access what each of these things mean. I am to find the meaning in each human interaction and I am able to finally begin to do that because with spiritual vision I am able to see the spirit within others that was hidden from me before. Another corner has been turned on my journey; I can't tell you when it happened, just that it did and it changes so many things.

I know this "life review" that I'm engaged in is vitally important and it is still unfolding and I will know when my search is at an end. At any given moment, I have no knowledge of where it will take me next, but I'm waiting for signs and listening for directions. I don't hear anyone say: *"Go here, or do this or that, etc."* but suddenly there is knowing and the path becomes clear.

I believe there are at least two aspects of this journey; one is to know myself and what meaning I have gained from my interactions with other spirits. The other is to know what meaning I have given to the lives of others.

I know that everything happens for a reason; there is a purpose behind all of it. I think it is so much more important to know what it means, than to seek to know why it happened.

This journey has not only taken me deep within myself, but deep inside others, to the place where their spirit dwells. I know it is important for me to know and understand who each spirit is in Truth. I have learned that no one is exactly as they appear on the surface. Each spirit is on it's own quest for Truth and we are all walking toward the same destination; even if we aren't aware of the journey and don't believe in the destination. I also know we will all arrive when it is our time and only when all have reached the destination will we be truly whole and at peace. May God bless you as you travel your own road home.

J.S. Schmidt

ACKNOWLEDGEMENTS

1. Sweet Holy Spirit................................Joe Isaacs

2. Letting Go..Paul McCartney

3. Sweet Inspiration..................Dan Penn/ Spooner Oldham

4. Rose-Colored Glasses...George F. Baker/ John W. Conlee

5. Do You Hear What I Hear.........Noel Regney/ Gloria Shane

6. Here, There, And Everywhere...J. Lennon/ P. McCartney

7. Like A Rock................................Bob Seger

8. The Weight................................ J. R. Robertson

9. Pretty Blue Eyes......Teddy Randazzo/ Bobby Weinstein

10. Heartaches By The Number...................Harlan Howard

11. Wreck Of The Edmund Fitzgerald...Gordon Lightfoot

12. Small Town..................................John Mellencamp

13. Among My Souvenirs......Edgar Leslie/Lawrence Wright

13. Cobwebs and Dust.........Gordon Lightfoot

14. For Whom The Bell Tolls...B. Gibb/R. Gibb/M. Gibb

15. Farewell Party.....................S.T. Lawton

                       M. Lawton

                       T. McKeehan

                       T. Rosenau

                       D. Wyall

                       N. D. Ready

                       D. Bullock

                       G. Patillo

                       B. Haley

16. Only The Good Die young.......................Billy Joel

17. Ring Them Bells................................Bob Dylan
18. Days of Future Passed...........J. Hayward
                                        M. Pender
                                        R. Thomas
                                        J. Lodge
19. Whispering Hope.......A. Hawthorn / D. Savino
20. Those were The Days............Gene Raskin
21. Dream On......................Steven Victor Tallerico
22. Where No One Stands Alone....Thomas Mosie Lister
23. He Stopped Loving Her Today...B. Braddock/C.Putman
24. What's Your Mama's Name?.D. Frazier/E. Montgomery
25. Sweet Dreams.................Don Gibson
26. Heavenly Sunshine..................................Cook/Zelley
27. Where Have All The Flowers Gone........Pete Seeger
28. You Say It's your Birthday.......J. Lennon/P. McCartney
29. Hear The Voice Of My Beloved...G. Gaither
                                        Wm J. Gaither
                                        R.P. Griffin
30. These Eyes.............B. Cummings/R. Bachman
31. Help Me Make It Through The Night...K. Kristofferson
32. Stepping In A Slide Zone...........J. C. Lodge
33. On The turning Away...........D. Gilmour/ A. Moore
34. Till I Can Make It On My Own.. B. Sherrill
                                        G. Richey
                                        T. Wynette
35. UnDun/ She's Come Undone... R. Bachman
36. It Don't Matter To Me...............David Gates
37. Have Thine Own Way....Adelaide A Pollard
38. Five Minutes...........................B.J. Duffy
                                        D. Greenfield
                                        H.A. Cornwell
                                        J.J. Burnel
39. Hooked On A Feeling...............Mark James

40. Old Dogs,Children And Watermelon Wine..T.T. Hall
41. Sweet Hour Of Prayer..............W.W. Walford
42. How Will I Know?....................S. Rubicam

                                                     G. Merrill

                                                N.M. Walden
43. Laughing........................B. Cummiings/ R. Bachman
44. Standing On The Promises...Russell K. Carter
45. How Deep Is Your Love...B.Gibb/R.Gibb/M.Gibb
46. Hard Day's Night.................J. Lennon/ P. McCartney
47. The Impossible Dream.......L. Mitch/D. Joseph
48. Lemon Tree...Will Holt
49. Laugh, Laugh..................................Ronald Elliott
50. Crying.............................J. Melson/ R. Orbison
51. Peace Train...Y. Islam